THE
ENLIGHTENED
CYCLIST

THE
ENLIGHTENED
CYCLIST

COMMUTER ANGST, DANGEROUS DRIVERS, AND OTHER OBSTACLES ON THE PATH TO TWO-WHEELED TRANSCENDENCE

BIKE SNOB NYC

CHRONICLE BOOKS
SAN FRANCISCO

DEDICATION:

To everybody everywhere who commutes by bicycle.

Library of Congress Cataloging-in-Publication Data available.

ISBN: 978-1-4521-0500-0

Manufactured in China

Designed by Michael Morris

10 9 8 7 6 5 4 3 2

Chronicle Books LLC
680 Second Street
San Francisco, California 94107
www.chroniclebooks.com

TABLE OF CONTENTS

A NOTE ON COMMUTING

Merriam-Webster offers the following definitions of commute (though not in this order):

- "to travel between back and forth regularly (as between a suburb and a city)"
- "to give in exchange for another"
- "to change (a penalty) to another less severe <commute a death sentence to life in prison>"

This book focuses on commuting, and when I use that word I often mean that first thing, which is going back and forth to your school or workplace.

However, I also use the word to include all forms of practical cycling and transportation in general—shopping, running errands, and even social calls—really, any trip in which the importance of the destination and what you do there trumps the journey itself. (As opposed to, say, putting on Lycra pants and riding just for the fun of it.)

In other words, if you don't go to school, you don't work, and you mostly go places by bike to drink beer with friends, you can still read this book.

Also, this is not a work of bicycle advocacy or a treatise on municipal traffic statutes. In fact, if you're looking for facts and statistics, you'd be better off buying a case of Snapple and reading the trivia on the underside of the bottle caps. So if you dropped out of school and don't like to use your brain, good, you can still read this book (or have a friend read it to you).

Additionally, when I refer to commuting, I'm also implicitly referring to that other definition: "to give in exchange for another." We generally experience frustration while commuting for one of two reasons: Either certain people want us to give in and exchange our vehicle type for another, or people don't want to make way for those who have elected to perform this exchange and use a vehicle type different from their own.

Last, while much of this book is about what's currently wrong with our approach to commuting and why, the ultimate goal relates to that last definition: "to change (a penalty) to another less severe." The way we commute can eventually change the misery that is inherent in our lives into something less severe and unpleasant, for ourselves and for others.

We're not our bikes, we're not our cars, and—thank freaking goodness—we are not our Segways. We are only ourselves.

INTRODUCTION:

COMMUTING BY BICYCLE AND THE INDIGNITY THEREOF

It is a summer afternoon on a weekday in Brooklyn. I am feeling irrationally optimistic (inasmuch as all optimism is irrational), and I am riding my bicycle from my home in an "uncool" neighborhood to a destination along the borough's "cool belt" (or, as I call it, the "Great Hipster Silk Route") roughly three miles away.

As I travel toward the more gentrified neighborhoods, New York City's nascent bicycle infrastructure literally materializes beneath my wheels in the form of lime green protected bike lanes and white chevron-shaped "sharrows." Whereas moments before, battered livery cabs and dilapidated minivans with duct-taped bumpers nearly forced me into parked cars, I'm now safely ensconced in my own lane and happily reciting that hoary Irish blessing (at least the part of it I know): "May the road rise to meet you, may the wind be ever at your back." My optimism borders on bliss.

As the sun shines warmly on my face, I stop at a red light, and as I watch the pedestrians strolling along the sidewalk on my right and the cars queuing on my left and the bicycle sharrows pointing ever forward to a glorious shared-road future, I catch myself thinking, "Maybe David Byrne and his friends are right and there is something to this whole 'livable streets' thing."

However, my joy is short-lived. First, the car in the queue on my left noses its way into the crosswalk in order to gain the crucial six-foot head start necessary to win the traffic-light drag race that occurs at every intersection. This causes anybody foolish enough to be traveling on foot to venture into oncoming traffic in order to ford the street. (This includes any children from the nearby school.) The driver cradles a cell phone to his ear, and his brake lights flash strobe-like with impatience as he inches forward. Behind him, each subsequent vehicle lines up a bit to the left or right of the one in front of it in an attempt to gain a line of sight or a potential holeshot. (Thanks to the advent of SUVs, minivans, and "crossover vehicles," it has been impossible for a driver to see over the top of another passenger car since the late 1980s.) Before long, this ragged assembly resembles a derailed train. In many places, this traffic meanders into the new bike lane and obstructs it.

It's not all impatience though. Some people do take advantage of red-light downtime, and occasionally an opaque-tinted window (illegal in my state yet ubiquitous nevertheless) rolls down so that the driver can eject a cigarette butt, wadded-up tissue, or empty beverage container. (While this sort of littering may sound offensive, it's what the people who don't roll down their illegally tinted windows might be doing in there that is worrisome. Hard drug use, routine firearm maintenance, and masturbation all leap to mind.)

Meanwhile, as I wait, I am joined by more cyclists. "Finally, my people!" I think to myself. However, instead of stopping behind me, or even next to me, the first rider comes to a stop in front of me. Then, the next one comes to a stop in front of her, and so forth, until they're practically blocking the intersection. The ones on fixed-gear bicycles attempt to trackstand, with varying degrees of success.

Somehow, even though I arrived at the light first, I'm now the last in line. It's almost as if all these other riders are participating in some kind of commuter "alleycat" (a "practicalitycat" perhaps?) and have conspired to block me in their quest for glory. However, apart from the fact that their helmets are similarly askew and their gluteal clefts are similarly exposed (much to the delight of the salacious driver doing who-knows-what behind his tinted windows), the cyclists all appear to be perfect strangers. They also look like a disheveled human chain attempting to cross a mighty river of motor vehicles, and whenever a gap opens up in perpendicular traffic, one of them leaps across, barely making it through alive.

The pedestrians, for their part, simply weave their way through the cars and trucks and bikes, too engrossed in their own cell-phone conversations, littering, and loogie-hocking to notice.

When the light finally changes to green, neither the crosswalk-blocking driver nor the remaining cyclists in front of me even notice, since their head start–gaining tactics have placed them too far underneath the traffic light to actually see it. Immediately, the racetrack fanfare of impatient car horns sounds, and the cyclists in front of me struggle to jab their feet into their wildly spinning toeclips (or to simply place their feet on their pedals if they are of the flat variety). I ride past them all at a leisurely pace and soon overtake the ones farther along who have just risked their lives for a now-moot seven-second head start.

Moments later, I arrive at the finish line of this urban drag race—the next red light, which is where every vehicle (both motorized and human-powered) inevitably winds up regardless of how fast or slow it was from the gun. The same cars line up next to me, and the same cyclists swarm in front of me, all simply hurrying up to wait once again, yet all apparently under the impression that it's somehow going to be different this time. This time, surely, one of them will "win" and live on forever as the Legend of Vanderbilt Avenue, fielding sexual advances and lucrative sponsorship offers for the rest of time. For me, however, all of it only serves to underscore the futility of life, and my optimism has yielded to pathos. The road has risen to meet me, and it has slapped me across the face.

Indeed, nobody is too dignified, too sensible, or even too responsible for the safety of others to participate in this race—and this includes city bus drivers. A few red lights later, I am the only cyclist at the intersection, and I hear a horn sound behind me. It is a city bus, and the driver is looking at me accusingly and pointing alternately at the red light and his own watch. Evidently, he is under the impression that I will somehow slow him down, and he wants me to get out of his way by running the light. Of course, my vehicle is to his lumbering autobus as a jet ski is to the QEII, and short of actually refusing to move at all there is absolutely no way I could possibly delay him. Briefly considering doing just this in order to spite him, I instead simply ride away when the light turns green. Naturally, by the time his last passenger has boarded the bus at the next corner, I'm four bus stops away.

On the way back home, a police car is obstructing the freshly painted bike lane that once gave me such exuberant hope. I assume the officer is monitoring the intersection for moving violations, but when a young gentleman wearing a Nazi-inspired helmet and riding a street-illegal 125cc two-stroke dirt bike runs the light by cutting through the gas station, the officer is singularly unconcerned. At the next red light, I find myself next to the motorcyclist, who points to the red light and says, "You got the light, bro." He then shrugs and runs it himself, turning the wrong way down a one-way street, apparently oblivious to the irony of both his riding style and his helmet, which evokes a political regime that would have happily gassed him. Also ironically, by the time I return to my bike-unfriendly neighborhood, the absence of any pretense that I belong on the road as a cyclist is almost a relief. A slap in the face hurts worse when it's preceded by a kiss.

Most ironic of all, though, is the fact that, despite the indignity of commuting by bicycle, I not only continue to do it, but also find it both practical and enjoyable. This is true of more and more people all over the country, and consequently many cities and towns are reworking their streets to accommodate them. In the meantime, though, the streets remain a place rife with indignity, as well as absurdity, conflict, misunderstanding, misfortune, and even death—for, as long as there are people, they will make poor decisions, and as long as there are vehicles, they will crash into each other.

We live in a country beset by many problems: a troubled economy; a lack of affordable health care; involvement in two wars; the constant specter of terrorism; and an overall decrease in the quality of our popular entertainment that is, quite frankly, staggering. Yet somehow, when the public discourse turns to something as seemingly innocuous as riding bicycles for transportation, people respond vociferously enough to make Mel Gibson blush. Radio DJs advocate running down cyclists; Critical Massers cry for "U-lock justice"; some say the United States should follow the leads of bike-friendly countries such as Holland and Denmark; others say bicycles should be banned altogether. And everyone, regardless of vehicle choice, recounts his or her own personal indignities and cites examples of why all other modes of transit are evil.

Yes, everybody's angry when it comes to commuting, and in a society in which racism is no longer acceptable, prejudice based on transport has rushed in to fill the void. But is there hope for the future? Are cyclists really saving the world? Are drivers really destroying it? Is one vehicle truly better than the other? And can't we all put aside our petty differences, join hands, and hate one thing together and in perfect harmony?

If you want the short version, the answers to the above questions are: Yes, No, No, That depends, and Mel Gibson. I believe that if we can figure out a way to emerge from the other end of our commute in a state of happiness, we can change the world.

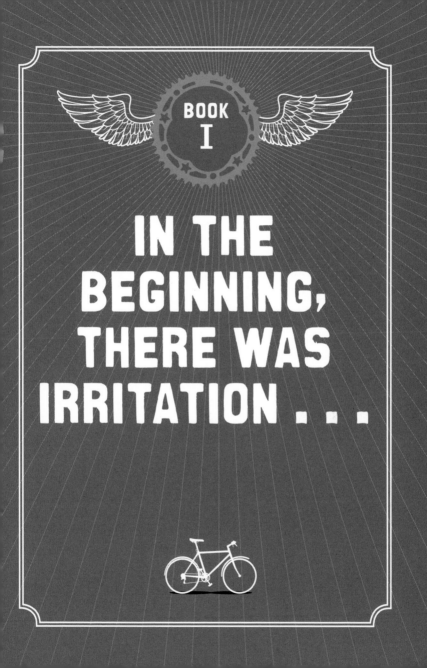

BOOK I

IN THE BEGINNING, THERE WAS IRRITATION . . .

REVELATION:

THE WORST DAY I EVER HAD AND WHY IT GAVE ME FAITH IN HUMANITY

Most New Yorkers remember exactly where they were when the World Trade Center was attacked on September 11, 2001, and I recall my exact whereabouts on that horrific morning as vividly as any moment in my entire life:

I was on the toilet.

Actually, I wasn't on the toilet until the second plane hit. I was having a quiet, media-free morning and had been unaware of the attack until the woman I was married to at the time, Tamara, called me from the West Side Highway in Manhattan. I was still at home in Brooklyn, and she was on the way back from dropping our dog off at the vet to have a tooth removed. She said there seemed to be some kind of giant fire downtown and that traffic was a mess.

Born in post–Robert Moses New York, I've been traveling the greater metropolitan area with one vehicle or another or by public transit my entire life. Some of my earliest memories are of approaching Manhattan from Queens by car, looking at that thrillingly imposing giant broken picket fence that is the skyline, and hearing my father ask, "Should we take the bridge or the tunnel?"

Of course, what he was asking me was: Which overture did I prefer? Did I want the drama and bombast of traveling beneath the girders and spires of the 59th Street Bridge, soaring across the East River, and dive-bombing into the city below? Or did I want the suspenseful droning of the Midtown Tunnel, monotonous and seemingly eternal, the humming of tires like the cosmic stirrings of the first movement of Beethoven's Ninth Symphony, until suddenly and without warning we exploded into daylight amid the skyscrapers in a burst of brass and tympana?

Years later, when I began to drive, my father modified the question slightly: "Will you take the bridge or the tunnel?" It was a subtle difference, but the change in meaning could not have been greater. What he was now asking was: Will you make the right choice? Will you try the bridge, which is free, but also a bit out of your way, and which could cost you an eternity of sitting in traffic? Or will you spend a precious Triborough Bridge and Tunnel Authority token on the tunnel, which will be well worth it if the tunnel is clear, but which will be a dear sacrifice if you end up inching your way through the tunnel sucking carbon monoxide, while a little farther uptown craftier drivers are zipping over the bridge without toll or hindrance?

All of this is to say that I come from a "Bridge and Tunnel" family, and just as the wild animal is eternally preoccupied with the source of his next meal, the bridge-and-tunneler is constantly managing his or her entrance to or egress from the city. We live and die by our route choice.

While the term "bridge and tunnel" is used disparagingly, the truth is that New York is much more than sophisticated Manhattan (and now the gentrified neighborhoods of Brooklyn). It is the bridges and tunnels, and the trains, and the buses, and the cultural relationships between "cosmopolitan" New York and the residential and suburban neighborhoods they connect. My route choice was not important to my father because he's some sort of paternal dictator, micromanaging my comings and goings; in fact, he's quite the opposite, and as a parent was and is always patient and benign. No, it was important to him because the New York City metropolitan area is vast, crowded, and complicated, and how you navigate it and by what means can be the difference between an expedient jaunt and an interminable, nightmarish slog. And of course, all of this is useless if you are unfamiliar with the subways and commuter trains and the ribbons of parkway and expressway that cover New York like so much spilled spaghetti, as well as the checkered tablecloth street grid beneath them. So, as the hunter teaches his son how best to fell the bison or the fisherman instructs on how best to angle for fish, so did my father endeavor to make me transit-savvy so I would grow to be hardy and able to effectively negotiate our challenging environment. To this day, he insists on knowing just how I will be getting to the airport, and if we are en route to the same destination, he will call me along the way and gloat if he gets there first. Woe unto the Weiss who is the last one to the seder, for the fleet of foot will bask in filial pride, while the sluggish shall feel only shame.

So when I got that call on the morning of September 11 about thick smoke and thicker traffic, I still had no idea the extent of the tragedy unfolding, since I had not yet turned on the TV. All I knew was that the car trip I had green-lit—consisting of an early morning departure toward Manhattan through the tunnel with a dog who was about to undergo dental surgery, concluding with a mid-morning return to Brooklyn going opposite the rush—was now going horribly awry. I thought of time being wasted in traffic and of doing a disservice to my family's tradition of deft trip-planning. In the remembering of a tragedy, it's the silly little things we were worried about immediately beforehand that emphasize its enormity. It's like worrying about a dripping faucet in the moments before you discover that a tsunami is heading toward your house.

After verbally navigating Tamara away from the situation, I turned on the television to find out what was going on, and then I adjourned to the restroom, where I could hear the newscaster talking about a fire at the World Trade Center and what witnesses were calling a plane crash. Then, as I sat, there was a boom, and the toilet seat vibrated beneath me, and the newscaster's voice became very agitated, and I might have laughed at the surreality of it all if it wasn't now completely clear to me that something truly horrible was happening. The newscaster was narrating something that was happening in downtown Manhattan, and here I was actually feeling it on the other side of New York Harbor—through a toilet seat. I now understood we were under attack, and I had quite literally been caught with my pants down.

Seconds later, I was on the phone again with Tamara; she had not managed to avoid the melee. Instead, she'd gotten off the West Side Highway and was now on Greenwich Avenue maybe eight blocks north of the Twin Towers.

In a city undergoing extreme emergency, there is no vehicle more cumbersome and useless than a car, as Tamara was now realizing.

Conversely, there is no better vehicle in this situation than a bicycle, and so I didn't need to give any thought as to what the fastest way to get to the World Trade Center would be. In moments, I was on my bike and racing to the Brooklyn Bridge. Though I was conscious of sirens and jet engines and helicopter blades, it didn't occur to me to actually look up until I was on the span of the bridge, at which point I saw the towers in flames for the first time.

As a child in Bayswater, Far Rockaway, at the very periphery of the city, I could see the Manhattan skyline across Jamaica Bay from the end of my block, looming and gray beyond the landfill, like a row of bad teeth. The city barely seemed real to me then—it was an Oz-like alternate reality in the distance, accessible only by those twin wormholes: the tunnel and the bridge. The Twin Towers were just a couple of years older than I was, and they were always the skyline's most visible element as I raced up and down the street on my bicycle. Now, here I was racing toward them as they burned. I thought about that as I climbed the span, and about all the people who were dying in them, and started to cry.

It wasn't until I was descending the span that I encountered the first wave of shocked people walking across the bridge from Manhattan to Brooklyn, and it occurred to me as I picked my way through them that I was the only person actually headed into the city—which, as I entered it, was not thrumming as it usually was, but was instead in a paradoxical state of both lethargy and panic. The shocked denizens of rush hour walked slowly, attempting to get cell phone signals, while people in FBI windbreakers ran around like it was a movie set and jet fighters scrambled overhead. When I finally reached Tamara, maybe fifteen minutes after leaving home, she was standing next to the car, and she and a group of stunned bystanders were simply staring at the sky. When I looked up too (for the second time that day), I could see what they had been watching all this time: people leaping from the flaming buildings to their deaths. It was the first time I ever saw anybody die.

The days immediately after September 11, 2001, were characterized by an extraordinary sense of goodwill. After all, most of us had never witnessed tragedy on this scale, and it was so enormous that it essentially short-circuited our usual suspicion and guile so that only compassion still functioned. Everywhere people lined up for blocks to donate blood, and it seemed as though every exchange between both neighbors and strangers took place in the spirit of mutual gratitude and respect. In a city where millions of people rub shoulders and fight for space every day, it's normal that a callus should develop over human interaction, but this tragedy essentially removed it and exposed the fundamental goodness and shared humanity that lie beneath. Eventually, the inevitable controversies and recriminations would reemerge, and a new callus would be formed. (Tamara and I would also divorce, and our dog would die of natural, nonterrorist causes.) But in those days, New York was a utopia of human compassion, albeit with a pit of fire right in its heart.

I think about that day all the time—especially when I commute. Not only because it was the most horrific, shocking, spectacular, and incomprehensible thing I've ever seen, but because when they are commuting people are very often at their worst. They will scream obscenities at each other, fight, and even blithely threaten each other's lives. But on September 11 and in the days that followed, when we lived in the middle of a war zone, you didn't hear so much as a car horn, let alone an obscenity.

When a driver intentionally swerves into me while I'm riding my bicycle, I try to assuage my rage by remembering that, beneath the callus, that compassion is still there. Granted, I'm not always successful, but nevertheless that knowledge has given me the strength to negotiate many frustrating situations—kind of like the way your job can seem just a little bit easier after you have a frank and intimate conversation with your boss.

You can learn a lot about a culture, and indeed about humanity, by exploring the manner in which people get around and the way they interact while doing so. It's when we're all on our way someplace to attend to our lives that the entire range of human behavior is on display—everything from the petty rage that consumes us when we feel affronted to the intense goodwill that subsumes us in the wake of a tragedy. As infuriatingly bad as our interactions on the street can be, it's essential to know that this compassion is what lies beneath our frustration. More than laws and better infrastructure and more bike lanes, it's getting in touch with that compassion and being able to draw upon it that will bring us the happiness that so often eludes us.

COMMUNION THROUGH COMMUTING:
WHY COMMUTING IS THE PORTAL AND THE BICYCLE IS THE TOOL

Our lives are an abstraction.

Consider the book you're reading. You may have a paper version perched atop your belly as you luxuriate in a hammock sipping a cocktail from a coconut. Or, perhaps you're reclined in your comfortably worn La-Z-Boy with some sort of e-book while the cat licks your feet. You may even be listening to it on a pair of headphones, as read by Ben Kingsley—if things turn out the way I hope they do, that is. (So far, Ben's not returning my messages, but if you're actually narrating this now, Mr. Kingsley, I hope you're using the same accent you used in *Sexy Beast*.)

Regardless of how you're reading this, though, even though I'm speaking directly to you (or through my proxy, Ben Kingsley) the very fact that you're able to do this shows just how abstract our lives have become. Many thousands of years ago, if I had wanted to share my thoughts on cycling with you, I would have had to come all the way to your cave and sit down with you over some smoked bison. Slightly more recently, I might have written them on parchment in hieroglyphics and then traded them to you for some indigo or a mummified cat for my pyramid to keep me comfortable in the afterlife. In the fifteenth century, things got much easier thanks to John Gutenberg's press, though there wasn't much demand for books, since only the nobility could afford them and only, like, nineteen people knew how to read anyway. Now, you grab a hunk of plastic that looks like a mouse, virtually press a bunch of pixels that look like a button, spend some money you'll never touch, and viola (I prefer viola to voilá since I don't speak French), you get a bunch of words. (Or you get Ben Kingsley reading you a bunch of words—or maybe a lesser Baldwin brother if the Kingsley thing didn't work out.)

Moreover, our lives are similarly abstracted in all sorts of other ways as well. Most of us don't grow, harvest, raise, hunt, or kill our food—we buy it. We don't need to go anywhere near a symphony hall (or a record store for that matter) to experience the transcendent beauty of Beethoven's Ninth. And between cell phones and computers and tablets and whatever other gewgaws are out there by the time you read this, we're really only a small handheld device away from actually being telepathic.

Still, there are certain fundamental aspects of our lives that remain, if not totally primal, more or less the same as they were millions of years ago when we first climbed down from the trees—or, if you're a creationist, thousands of years ago when we first materialized in a Middle Eastern garden. (Some creationist accounts put Earth at about ten thousand years old, which means it's actually slightly younger than agriculture and pottery.) Despite the Barry

White soundtrack, sex is still sex. Despite the epidural and fertility treatments, childbirth is still childbirth. And, most important to this book, despite the sheer variety of routes and vehicles available to us, getting from one place to another is still getting from one place to another.

This is because, beneath all the refinements, our motivations for engaging in these things and the feelings they arouse in us remain essentially unchanged. We'll always experience the headiness of lust and arousal, and no matter how clinical and closely monitored, the process of childbirth will always seem miraculous and filled with that exquisitely terrifying combination of fear and joy. Similarly, we'll always be compelled to travel, and our journeys today are fraught with the same psychological implications as they were ten thousand years ago when Adam and Eve stumbled out of the Garden of Eden and into some Stone Ager's potato patch.

This is because whenever we set out on a journey—whether it's a trip around the world or a simple commute to work—there's always the possibility that something unexpected will happen. This is also why when we set off on a journey there's always some degree of apprehension and fear, even if we're barely aware of it.

Consider our primitive ancestors (or at least the caricature of them I'm about to cobble together). They would have left their caves each morning in search of water and brontosaurus meat and bison-fur unitards and other Stone Age necessities with a considerable amount of trepidation, for they were venturing into a Great Wide World fraught with mystery and peril. Enemy clans, saber-toothed tigers, and swooping pterodactyls were just a few of the things they were likely to encounter—and this is to say nothing of tar pits and quicksand and poisonous plants and dragonflies the size of recumbent bicycles. This is why they armed themselves with clubs, which they used to defend themselves from hostile clans and giant insects, as well as for making marriage proposals, since "romance" wasn't invented until the first century B.C. (and it wasn't perfected until Barry White released his first solo album in 1973).

Today, little has changed. Sure, we have bicycles and cars and trains and paved roads lined with Starbucks now, but we still venture off into a potentially hostile world, and we carry in our panniers and briefcases that mix of apprehension and fear. This is because modern society is a lot like the sitcom *The Young Ones*, only with a seemingly infinite number of roommates, and as soon as we step out of our respective bedrooms into the universally shared living room that is the Great Wide World, we are at each other's mercy. There's never any guarantee that one of our roommates won't eat all of our snack foods, commandeer the TV, or hit us in the head with a 2 x 4 for some canned laughter and applause. This is why we're almost always on the defensive when we commute. We're never quite sure who's going to be out there or just how big of an asshole he or she might be.

Most important, let's not forget that absolutely anything can happen to us out there in the Great Wide World, even on the most mundane journey. It's as true now as it was in the Stone Age. On September 11, as I was watching people leap to their deaths, all I could think about was that the only thing these people had done this morning was get up and go to work. They weren't combatants, or political radicals, or religious zealots. These weren't people putting their lives at risk for recreation or work—hardcore backpackers lighting out on exotic trips in blithe disregard of State Department travel advisories or underwater welders setting off to work on oil rigs in the Gulf of Mexico for danger pay. They weren't even fabled Dog Whisperer

César Millán, who probably embarks upon his commute knowing all too well that any day he could wind up getting mauled to death by a spoiled Pomeranian. If anything, when these moribund people's alarms went off that morning, they probably thought to themselves what most of us do when we get up, which is some variation of "same shit, different day." They showered, they got in cars, they boarded trains, they unfurled folding bicycles, and they headed off to yet another day at the office—only to find themselves confronting not drudgery, but horror. And standing on a ledge and deciding whether to die by inferno or self-defenestration.

We rarely think consciously about this possibility when we set out in the morning, but it's true for all of us, no matter where we live. The flooding in New Orleans; the earthquakes in California; the tsunamis in Asia. The difference between the mundane and the epic is just a tiny bit of happenstance.

This is why even an ostensibly normal day of commuting can be disastrous or deadly. The commuting theater is the Great Wide World, the last bastion of unabstracted human interaction and exposure to limitless potential for happenstance. The white "ghost bikes" I see all over the city attest to this. So do all the car crashes on the highway you'll hear about on the traffic report as a matter of routine. In fact, they're so routine that they're expected, and the traffic report only mentions these crashes so that we can circumvent and ignore them. Even in a big city like New York, a crime is newsworthy, but an injury or death during rush hour is unremarkable—it's just an "accident." Commuting is one of the only arenas of life in which we're willing to accept sudden death at the hands of another human being.

All of this is also the reason that, in our highly refined and abstracted age, the simple business of getting from one place to another is one of the remaining areas of life in which a perfect stranger might scream at another. I'm not talking about Internet flaming, either; I'm talking about getting right up in someone's face, and calling them a "cocksucker." You'd never contemplate such a thing at a party, or in class, or at work (unless your goal was to be fired in truly epic and cinematic fashion). You wouldn't do it in a restaurant, or in a supermarket, or even while playing football. Maybe—maybe—you'd do it in a bar, but only because you were really drunk. But while commuting, people do this sort of thing all the time, whether it's from behind the wheel or behind the handlebars of a bicycle. We bark at each other like dogs. Even though one person may be driving some leather-upholstered pinnacle of German engineering and another may be riding some exquisitely lugged artisanal North American Handmade Bike Show masterpiece, this whole business of getting from one place to another is primal, and our vehicle choice seems to matter more than our humanity.

If some kind of messiah were to come to us and teach us all how to relate to each other with love and compassion and guide us to a higher plane of existence in which respect were to replace conflict and love were to supplant irritation, I have my theories about where he or she would arrive.

Think about it—would this messiah really arrive in the Middle East, where religious wars have been the order of the day since hummus was invented? Certainly not—past would-be messiahs have not fared well there (take Jesus for example) and there's no reason to think things would turn out better now.

Would he arrive in an impoverished, diseased, and war-torn African nation? Unlikely, since Bono, Angelina Jolie, and George Clooney would almost certainly resent the intrusion and do whatever it took to eject him so that the spotlight remained on them. "If anyone's going to go down as the messiah," you can almost hear Bono snarling in his Irish brogue as the would-be savior's panicked breath steamed up his human fly glasses, "it damn well better be me."

No, if the messiah really wanted the attention of the common person, and if he didn't want to be crucified as a blasphemer or bumped from his slot on Letterman by a celebrity philanthropist, then he or she should almost certainly arrive in a North American city during rush hour. As Jesus famously explained when he got caught dining with tax collectors, prostitutes, Goldman Sachs executives, and other sinners, "It is not the healthy who need a doctor, but the sick." Sure, this is the kind of thing you can imagine a politician saying upon getting caught playing "naughty nurse" with his mistress, but if we're to take Jesus at his word, he does make a good point. There's a reason you don't find sober people on *Celebrity Rehab with Dr. Drew*. Drug-addled celebrities make for good reality television, and wretched sinners make for good spiritual transformations.

This is why rush hour is ripe for a messiah. In what other arena are the rich and the poor, the driver and the cyclist, the user of public transit and the pedestrian all interacting, sharing space, and shouting "Cocksucker!" at one another in a deafening cacophony of fellatio?

The messiah's not going to appear in a Starbucks, as a bunch of people wait patiently for their venti soy lattes. Certainly, this enlightened being won't show up at the Apple store, where he or she would barely command the attention of the shoppers rapt in the creative possibilities of the new iMac or the magic of the iPad. (Steve Jobs has the "messiah" market cornered where Apple consumers are concerned, anyway.)

No, the messiah is going to appear at the busiest intersection in town, and he's either going to resurrect the cyclist who has just been run down by a driver on a cell phone, or miraculously pry some pregnant woman out of the twisted chassis of her T-boned Volkswagen, or simply wave a hand that shuts down every engine and freezes every bicycle drivetrain and silences all the shouts of "Cocksucker!" so that, in a moment of silence we've never before experienced, we remember that whatever we're doing and wherever we're all going, we all want the same thing:

To be happy, and to not get killed.

This is as close to the meaning of life as I think we're ever going to get. I don't know about you, but it's good enough for me.

We can't control earthquakes or tsunamis or even terrorist attacks, but we can at least exert some degree of influence over the rest of it. We don't have to call each other "cocksucker," and indeed a lot of the time we don't even really have to crash into each other. Sure, accidents do happen, but just how accidental is rear-ending someone because you were on your cell phone or crashing your bike because you were riding the wrong way down a one-way street at night without using lights?

In a larger sense, changing the way we commute is really the best opportunity we have to try to effect change for the better—not just by avoiding "accidents," but by generally practicing compassion and treating others well. Changing the way you commute is more effective than signing an online petition, or buying one product over another because it's "green," or even voting for one politician over another. Our commute is the void between our homes and our jobs and our recreation and our socializing—all arenas in which mutual respect and compassion are (ideally) already the norm—and if we can fill that void with benevolence instead of indifference, we can embark upon our commute with excitement instead of apprehension and emerge on the other side of it even happier than we were when we started. We don't even need bike lanes or federal funds or more efficient vehicles for that—we can do it using exactly what we have. I really believe we can commute ourselves to enlightenment.

CHOSEN COMMUTER

So where does the bicycle enter into this? Well, I believe the bicycle occupies a unique position in the Great Wide World, as do the people who ride it. In fact, I might even go so far as to call cyclists the "Chosen Commuters"—not because we're better, but because we have an important perspective and occupy a crucial vantage point, and when you're able to see something that others cannot or will not, then sometimes you're obligated to do something about it. For example, if you lived in a house with a river view and you saw someone dumping toxic chemicals into it every night, you wouldn't have to be an environmentalist to report them, you'd just have to be a decent person. It's the same with cyclists—we see what everybody's up to, and our perspective is important for the following reasons.

We Choose the Way We Commute

Most people choose their commuting method by default—they use a car because everyone else does where they live, or they use a train or bus because that's what's available to them. Cyclists on the other hand tend to commute by bicycle because we enjoy it, which means we're already predisposed to becoming benevolent commuters since we already understand the potential for our commute to bring us happiness. If you're looking to find happiness through commuting, you're more likely to get good advice from a cyclist, in the way that if you're looking for a good bakery you could probably do a lot worse than to ask a stoner.

We Are Slower than Cars but Faster than Pedestrians

When you drive a car you can't really make sense out of other commuters' behavior since either you're whizzing by them or else you're stuck in traffic and they're whizzing by you. Even your fellow drivers just exist theoretically inside giant exoskeletons, and you really only notice other road users when they're annoying you. On the other hand, when you're a pedestrian, you're generally occupying space reserved for foot traffic, and so pretty much any vehicle that violates that space is going to be piloted by a maniac. Cyclists, however, understand both sides. We are both menaced by cars and menacing to pedestrians, and we also have to be equally wary of both. Like cars, we use the streets, and like pedestrians, we are completely exposed. We are the omniscient commuters.

Cyclists Also Drive and Walk

Okay, we don't all drive, but many of us do, or at least we have at one time or another, being the products of a car-centric society that we are. We're also more likely to be comfortable with walking, since we're generally more physically active than your average car commuter. Conversely, plenty of drivers haven't used a bicycle since they were ten, and only walk to and from their cars. We all have our vehicular alliances, but generally speaking cyclists are more accepting of the idea of total commuter integration.

Nobody Likes Us

It's hard to be truly compassionate if you don't know what it feels like to be disliked. Cyclists do not have this problem, because nobody likes us. Drivers think we're smug dorks who slow them down, pedestrians think we're deadly scofflaws, and neither of them has much trouble imagining a world without us. Meanwhile, only the most extreme cyclists would advocate for a car- and pedestrian-free world. In this sense, we've got the most to lose.

The challenge then is to be the best cyclists we can, to rise above the primal nature of commuting, and conquer this Last Frontier of Hostility and Indifference. At the same time, we've also got to avoid the pitfall of vehicular prejudice, since this is the one aspect of commuting that is abstracted—in the chaos, we reduce drivers to their cars and cyclists to their bicycles. However, this only serves to exacerbate our mutual hostility, since divorcing a person from his or her humanity in a primal situation can be disastrous. It just places us at greater remove from our own compassion. Without compassion there's no empathy, and with no empathy there's only indifference. If we can rise above the fray, then I believe we can render the common experience that is the Great Wide World into a place you'd actually like to spend your time.

But first, we need a little background.

SMUGNESS

Merriam-Webster defines smugness as "an often unjustified feeling of being pleased with oneself or with one's situation or achievements." As cyclists, we are especially susceptible to this condition. There are three main reasons for this:

1. You power a bicycle yourself.
2. Bicycles are "green."
3. Bicycles are considered an "alternative" form of transportation.

Each of these factors independently has the power to make someone feel special, but if you've got all three, it's almost inevitable. You start to feel like some all-powerful wizard. This could explain why so many smug cyclists wear beards.

Smugness can take root in almost any climate, though it takes on different characteristics depending on the conditions. In Portland, Oregon, where the climate is moist and mild, the smugness is lush, and it manifests itself in exquisite handmade commuter bikes, artisanal accessories, and constant theme rides. In Minneapolis, where the winters are harsh, cyclists express their smugness by commuting in miserable conditions and proudly displaying the ice chips in their beards. And in New York, smugness takes the form of leaving your Range Rover out in the Hamptons and "portaging" your children to private school in an authentic *Bakfiets* bigger than most people's apartment.

Speaking of "portaging," that's just smug for "carrying stuff on a bike," and it is the ultimate expression of smugness. Birds puff up their feathers to attract a mate, and smug cyclists display their payloads to show how righteous they are and to complement their expensive cargo bikes. Indeed, at its core, smugness is really about doing something lots of people do, only while making a big deal about it and spending a bunch of money.

The degree to which someone does this can be expressed in their "Smugness Quotient," and to determine this quotient you simply apply the following formula:

PRICE OF BICYCLE / WEIGHT OF CARGO = SMUGNESS QUOTIENT

Using this formula, carrying twenty pounds of organic produce on a $2,899 Bakfiets would yield a smugness quotient of 144.95 (extremely smug), whereas carrying fifty pounds of recycling on a $25 old crappy ten-speed would give you a smugness quotient of 0.5 (negligibly smug).

GENESIS:
WHO WE ARE, HOW WE GOT THIS WAY, AND HOW TO GET TO WHERE WE NEED TO BE

As an auto mechanic can learn much about a motor's condition from the color of a spark plug or as an arborist can tell a tree's age by counting the rings (though this involves sawing down the tree, which sort of makes its age irrelevant), so we can learn much about our society from our commute. The way we get around and how we behave toward one another as we do speaks volumes about us as people. The Cliffs Notes of these volumes would basically read:

"We are a bunch of impatient assholes."

If we're going to change our nasty commuting habits and stop being unpleasant people most of the time, then we first have to learn how we got here and understand why we've become the commuters and the people we are today. Indeed, the manner in which we travel to and fro is imprinted on our cultural DNA, and the double helix of this DNA is an incredibly long ladder that we have been building over the entire course of human history, comprised of events and people, both real and imagined. At a certain point, the distinction between fact and fiction becomes irrelevant. Actually, in our culture fiction can be *more* powerful than fact. Consider religion and the wars it has caused, or the plays of Shakespeare, which we draw upon and reference as readily as any actual occurrence. Our cultural DNA is made up of our *complete* cultural history.

In order to sequence this DNA and figure out who we are, we must start at the beginning. But when was the beginning exactly? Well, some cultures use the Gregorian calendar, others use the Chinese lunar calendar, and still others the Hebrew calendar. There are even people who don't use calendars at all and simply live day-to-day, like freegans and marijuana enthusiasts. I, however, prefer to use my own metric, and I have devised a chronological measuring system that we can all employ. Free from the baggage of cultural bias, it is called the Dachshund of Time, and we can use it to summarize every epoch of human history.

To start, let's travel back to the time of the biblical prophets, who were the very first commuters and who set the moral trends many of us follow to this day.

BIBLICAL TIMES

While actual human history probably began millions of years ago when some primate figured out how to walk upright and use snappy catchphrases, from a Western cultural perspective, it all started in the Garden of Eden, when God made Adam and then went ahead and made Eve out of Adam's superfluous rib. All of this happened long before God retired, stopped talking to us, and abandoned us to our fate, which happened somewhere around the Dachshund of Time's groin area.

Things were much simpler back at the dawn of time, for while today it can take almost a week to get a pair of pants dry-cleaned, it took God only seven days to create the entire world—and that's factoring in the rest day.

It probably won't surprise you to learn that the concept of marketing is almost as old as humanity itself, and while I'll get into more detail on that later in this book, suffice to say here that it took almost no time for a wily serpent to sell Adam and Eve on a shiny apple from the Tree of Knowledge, at which point they became not only the first humans but also the first marketing demographic, and God expelled them from the Garden of Eden for being total consumerist dupes.

Thus expelled from Paradise, Adam and Eve and their descendants were essentially cursed. No more would people live a peaceful, carefree, naked existence in a beautiful garden bursting forth with organic, locally grown produce. Instead, men would have to toil over the land in order to feed themselves and their families, and women would have to experience excruciating pain in childbirth. Most important, they would also be commuters forevermore, bouncing miserably from crappy city to crappy city. And so, the pattern was set: a life of drudgery interspersed with lots of commuting (or, as they called it back then, schlepping.) In this sense, eating from the Tree of Knowledge was the Original Commuting Sin, and we've been paying for it ever since.

And it only got worse. After leaving Egypt, Moses and his people endured a forty-year commute, starting with a truly epic crossing of the Red Sea (which made getting through the Lincoln Tunnel at rush hour seem like traipsing across a country bridge in a sundress on a spring afternoon). When people did settle, their cities soon became awful places thanks to urban sprawl, and everyone kept having to abandon their homes due to God's wrath, commuting somewhere else to start over. Sodom, for example, got so bad that the people who lived there actually tried to rape a couple of visiting angels—which was frowned upon even in those wild times. This compelled God to destroy Sodom, and He even turned Lot's wife, Sarah, into a pillar of salt just for turning around and giving the place one last look.

But surely the commute that defines the era was Noah's voyage aboard his eponymous ark, and to this day it remains the most epic commuting story ever told.

As most people know, God felt that Earth had essentially "jumped the shark" (or "raped the angel" as they used to say back then), so rather than try to fix it, He instead decided to simply wash everyone away in a great flood and start over from scratch—just as you might do to your computer's hard drive if it has a really bad virus. So God spoke to Noah and commanded him to build an ark, aboard which he'd carry two of every animal in the world. (Ideally they were supposed to be male and female pairs so they could reproduce, but animal genitalia can be confusing, and there's no telling how many species were lost because of Noah's poor animal-sexing skills.) In this sense, the ark was like a portable computer hard drive and Noah was a one-man Geek Squad, and he dumped God's most important

THE DACHSHUND OF TIME

BIBLICAL TIMES

OLDEN DAYS

OLD SCHOO

files onto it before he zorched the virus-ridden computer that was the world.

Thus was born humankind's lust for gigantic vehicles, for God's instructions to Noah were basically the world's first car commercial, and the sales pitch was this:

Large vehicles are your salvation.

Yes, if your car is big enough, you will be safe as the wretched masses drown. To this day, consumers are attracted to giant, impractical vehicles, often citing the fact that they feel safer because they can see over traffic—that flood of lesser vehicles that never recedes. What is a minivan or SUV if not a modern-day ark? Indeed, the Dodge Grand Caravan with a religious-themed bumper sticker and a payload of rambunctious children is the vehicular descendant of Noah's ark just as surely as the bird is the evolutionary descendant of the dinosaur (if I may go so far as to evoke the Bible and evolution in the same sentence). In fact, given the biblical basis for large cars, I'm surprised manufacturers don't measure their SUVs in cubits and tout preparedness for the coming apocalypse as a selling point. This is also why drivers of large vehicles tend to be inconsiderate of other road users such as cyclists—they are the righteous ones, and you on your ridiculously puny contraption are just a hopeless sinner drowning in a sea of wretched humanity.

Anyway, eventually the flood waters did recede, and like a celestial Bill Gates or Steve Jobs (depending on your worldview) God relaunched the world as "Earth 2.0."

Of course, farther along on the Dachshund's rump, many years or prophets or Bible chapters later, Jesus tried to turn the whole "big car" thing on its ear—or, more accurately, its ass—by famously commuting into Jerusalem on a donkey which may or may not have had the world's first "Jesus fish" on it. An accessible, easily ridden, yet sluggish mode of transportation, the donkey was arguably the Dutch city bike of its day, and indeed it's not unreasonable to believe that Jesus might have ridden an actual bicycle if only the technology had been available at the time, for the evidence is overwhelming. Consider the following:

1. Jesus had a beard. People with beards love bicycles, as is clear to anybody who's visited a gentrified urban neighborhood or attended any sort of "bike culture" event. Some recumbent bicycle enthusiasts actually go so far as to claim that Jesus would have ridden a recumbent, but this is unlikely since his beard was of insufficient length. Also, he died in his early thirties, which is an extraordinarily young age for recumbent ownership, even by biblical standards.

2. Jesus was crucified mostly for being a nice guy. Then as now, people in authority hate people with beards who go around telling people to be nice to each other, since they find them intolerably smug. Furthermore, the bicycle just happens to be the most smug vehicle ever invented, which is why it is favored by people with beards who like to tell other people what to do. Sure, we live in much milder times now, so instead of crucifying them, we simply throw them in jail for participating in Critical Mass, but the idea is the same.

3. Jesus told a parable about a Good Samaritan. Most of us are familiar with the parable of the Good Samaritan,

in which one commuter helps another commuter who has been left for dead at the side of the road. Among cyclists, it is customary to stop and offer help when you see another cyclist whose bicycle is disabled or who appears to have been involved in a crash, a behavior that is almost unheard of among motorists. Certainly then, when you consider this, and the beard, and the smugness, it's almost certain that the historical Jesus would have ridden a bicycle.

Not that any of this should matter, mind you, since Jesus and his exploits have been used to justify far too many dubious endeavors—he's been used as the basis for everything from religious wars to Cadbury Creme Eggs. Nevertheless, there's no getting away from the fact that Jesus as portrayed in the Gospels sounds uncannily like a bicycle advocate, from the sandals all the way to the people turning on him for doing nothing more than putting forth a few good ideas.

Anyway, as the biblical era winds down, Saul changes his name to Paul and delivers a bunch of epistles (epistles are pretentious letters) all over the Mediterranean area, and like Jesus he almost certainly would have ridden a bicycle, though he probably would have ridden a fixed-gear and worn a messenger bag since he spent so much time delivering stuff. Ultimately, the Bible ends with a bunch of threats about the arrival of the Four Horsemen of the Apocalypse, who represent the final reckoning, or else the advent of the "hipster" culture, depending on who you ask.

THE OLDEN DAYS

As we move forward along the Dachshund of Time, away from the tail and toward the snout, we leave the biblical age and transition into the Olden Days. Mostly bereft of miracles and improbabilities like women made from ribs and people who talk to burning bushes and live until they're five hundred, the Olden Days were a far more prosaic time in which commuting began to more closely resemble the tedious back-and-forth style we practice today, only on a much larger scale. The defining—and most unpleasant—commute of this era was known as "The Crusades."

In the Olden Days, people were loaded with religious baggage, thanks to all the stuff that happened (or was supposed to have happened) back in Biblical Times. (It seems they took a lot of those stories *way* too seriously.) First, there was the Original Commuting Sin we're all born with, thanks to Adam and Eve. Second, there were all the different religious beliefs that had emerged from various interpretations of the Bible and the conflicts that resulted from them.

Some of these people happened to be very enthusiastic followers of the prophet Mohammed, and they commuted all over Asia and Europe and sort of "gentrified" different neighborhoods—though whereas now gentrification means renting a cheap apartment and opening a used record store, back then it meant arriving with an army and killing everybody who refused to follow your religion. One of the places they gentrified was Jerusalem, which was an extremely trendy city at the time and sort of the Williamsburg, Brooklyn, of its day—except instead of attracting indie bands it attracted religious cults.

Meanwhile, other people were followers of Jesus, having been very impressed by his friendly demeanor, his miracles, his beard, his famous donkey commute, and his general indie vibe. These people called themselves Christians, and for about two hundred years they traveled back and forth from Europe to Jerusalem as well—except instead of just hanging around, browsing the record stores, and glomming the free wi-fi in the local coffee shops, they tried to kill all the Muslims and make them leave. One way the Christians tried to get rid of the Muslims was by laying siege to Jerusalem. A siege is when you block vital goods from entering a city in order to weaken it, and the Crusaders' siege of Jerusalem would be like surrounding modern-day Williamsburg and blocking all shipments of tattoo ink, fair trade coffee, and recreational drugs. As you can imagine, the consequences would be devastating.

Needless to say, the Crusades, which spanned about three centuries, were a total bloodbath. This is because both sides claimed to have God in their corner—though God Himself, who talked incessantly back in Biblical Times, remained conspicuously silent. Not only that, but one might argue that the Crusades never ended, given terrorism, and September 11, and war in the Middle East, and all the rest of it. On the positive side though, all that intercontinental commuting to kill did cause trade to flourish, thanks to all the people commuting back and forth between Europe and the Middle East. It revitalized routes that had not been used for a very long time, and it also helped bring Europe out of the Dark Ages and into the Renaissance, otherwise known as the "Medieval Woodstock."

OLD SCHOOL

As we get to about the middle of the Dachshund of Time, we arrive in the Old School days. While things like owning other people, beating children, and beating other people were still common

WHY THE MESSENGER IS VAUNTED IN OUR CULTURE

Our culture isn't informed only by Judeo-Christian stories and traditions. Of equal if not more importance are the contributions of the ancient Greeks, who gave us philosophy, democracy, naked sporting events, and the eponymous Greek salad, among other things. (They even gave us the word eponymous.) Consequently, we also have much to learn from the ancient Greeks about the way we commute today, and while the biblical Paul may have been a proto—bike messenger, it's really the ancient Greeks whom you should thank for the liberal arts graduate with dreadlocks who almost runs you over when you cross the street during your lunch hour.

As anybody who's seen the original *Clash of the Titans* movie knows, the ancient Greeks worshipped many gods and were also plagued by claymation monsters. In many ways, these gods were personifications of our own lives and human nature: there were Aphrodite, the goddess of love and beauty; Ares, the god of war; and their son, Eros, who was also a love god, like his mother. (The ancient Greeks were an amorous people.) Later, the Romans also worshipped these gods, though they gave them different names for trademark reasons—Aphrodite became Venus, Ares became Mars, Eros became Cupid, and so forth. In other words, they took the same basic idea and changed it slightly, kind of like Microsoft did with the iPod when they released the Zune.

Anyway, one of these Greek gods was Hermes (or, if you prefer the Microsoft version, Mercury). Hermes was the messenger of the gods, and he used to wear very trendy winged boots and carry messages from Olympus to the humans. He also used to show dead people the way around the underworld. He was an athletic guy with a fondness for practical jokes. On top of all that, the Greeks even credited Hermes for inventing the lyre, which probably meant the actual human inventor, George Lyre, never received any royalties. And if that weren't enough, the Greeks also used to make sacrifices to Hermes before setting out on journeys due to his swift nature, accurate sense of direction, and general savoir faire. Now we have tollbooths and fare cards, but back then you had to burn a lamb before setting out on your commute.

So ingrained in our consciousness is this image of the insouciant, mischievous, rebellious, lyre-strumming, fleet-footed messenger that many people continue to venerate him in his current form—the bicycle messenger. Like Hermes, bicycle messengers are fast, they know their way around, and they have a sort of mischievous, daredevil appeal. Of course, the main difference is that they ride bikes, machines of which the ancient Greeks couldn't possibly have conceived, but if they had, it's entirely possible that Hermes would have opted for one instead of—or in addition to—his winged boots.

Oddly, though, this appreciation for the bicycle messenger just doesn't extend to people who make a living delivering other things by bicycle.

Consider food delivery people, for example. It's just as dangerous as delivering envelopes and modeling portfolios, and in fact when you really think about it, it's even more difficult, since a roast chicken or a pizza pie is generally more unwieldy than, say, an envelope containing a contract or a check. Not only that, but delivering food is technically more "anti-establishment" than being a bike messenger. Bike messengers are generally delivering for the law firms, financial companies, and giant corporations who profit from our misery, and for the fashion houses, advertisers, and glossy publications who brainwash us into spending our meager earnings on crap that's beyond our means. Plus, they do so for little money and no benefits—they're virtually slaves to the system. Meanwhile, most food delivery people are carrying nourishing food from independently owned restaurants to hungry working people who are too busy to cook. What's more, food delivery people even get tips, whereas the only tip a bike messenger gets is, "Take a shower."

So why are messengers rock stars, while food delivery people are merely seen as the busboys of the road?

Is it because messengers are often privileged people with edgy fashion sense and racing bicycles, whereas food delivery people are usually hardworking immigrants who tend not to spend their hard-earned wages on whisky shots and enhancements to their tattoo sleeves? Sure, to an extent, but that's really only a small part of it. In fact, since the messenger industry is constantly shrinking, trendy white people who want to ride bikes for a living are increasingly gravitating to the food delivery industry. Plus, in places like Portland they're delivering not only traditional takeout but also soup, fair trade coffee, beer, and even Christmas trees (though obviously those are for decorating, not for eating). Entrepreneurial? Absolutely. Convenient? Certainly yes. Smug? Without question. Cool in that rebellious "I don't need society" kind of way? Absolutely not—I couldn't care less about what's cool, but I do know it when I see it, and there's absolutely nothing cool about soup tureens.

No, in the end it all comes down to archetypes, Joseph Campbell, and our collective consciousness; the simple fact is that our collective consciousness collectively decided millennia ago that messengers are cool. They carried messages across battlefields; they were privy to the king's secrets, yet not bound by the physical confines of his court; and eventually people sublimated their admiration for them into the messenger god Hermes. Meanwhile, there's no food delivery god, nor did the ancient Greeks worship a deity who pushed a snack cart up and down Mount Olympus. They only worshipped the people who actually did the eating, like Dionysus, the Greek god of feasting, drinking, and generally partying self-indulgently. Sure, this does not speak well of us, but this is how we are, and our worship of Hermes and Dionysus yesterday has resulted in our obsession with messengers and celebrities today.

practice, thanks to the Renaissance, people were slowly becoming more enlightened and were coming to terms with certain truths that seem obvious to us now—facts like that the Earth is round and that it revolves around the Sun. Sure, the average person still thought the Moon was made of cheese and that one day humankind would reach it and turn it into the biggest fondue pot in the universe, but on the whole, things are starting to look familiar by this point.

Our newfound understanding of geography had a huge impact on commuting, which still took place on an epic scale and was still drenched in blood. Most notably, the Old School era was the time of the Great Explorers, who discovered entirely new continents—though the fact that they were new did come as a surprise to the people who had already been living on them for millions of years. Also surprising were all the bacteria and viruses the Great Explorers and their crews brought along with them, which wiped out countless people. If all this weren't bad enough, the explorers had the temerity to call these people *Indians*, which is like someone calling you by the name of a distant cousin you've never met as they rob your house and kick your dog.

Soon enough, ships from Europe began commuting to and from this so-called New World, and the commute eventually evolved into the "triangle trade." Yes, Crusading was "out," and Trading was "in." This three-way commute worked as follows:

- The Europeans sailed to Africa and traded a bunch of trinkets for actual human people.
- Next, the Europeans went to the New World, where they sold the people.

- Finally, they loaded up on New World goodies like rum, sugar, and tobacco, which they brought back to Europe. Ironically, this stuff wound up killing Europeans just like their germs had killed the Indians, albeit more slowly, and indeed it's still killing us today.

Like the Crusades, Old School commuting was a pretty miserable affair all around, but also like the Crusades, we owe our current way of life to it, for better and for worse. Most important, the world became "smaller" than it had ever seemed before, since by sailing all over it we were finally able to wrap our minds around it. No longer was it this slab off of which you'd fall if you sailed too far. Moreover, as we began to compartmentalize the world and as various classes of people began to emerge, the template was set for the sort of commuting we practice today.

BACK IN THE DAY

Once we arrive at Back in the Day, that colorful period right behind the Dachshund of Time's floppy ears, the world is, for the most part, very recognizable. Back in the Day is a vital period of human history, because without it we would not be able to make other people feel wimpy and inferior. "You know, back in the day we didn't have things like seatbelts and vaccines," your great-grandfather might tell you as he pops an entire unshucked oyster into his mouth and devours it like a granola bar. Also, unlike the other periods, which are fixed in time, Back in the Day is more subjective in that it's basically the time period before the one we're in now—in other words, today plus time and inconvenience equals Back in the Day.

It's not terribly hard to imagine what things were like Back in the Day, since between your great-grandfather's stories, Westerns, and TV shows like *Mad Men*, you've probably got a pretty good idea of what the past one hundred years looked like. By this point, all the exploration and colonialism that characterized the Old School period had petered out, mostly due to the fact that we ran out of places to explore and colonize and just wound up fighting each other, after which the people who were living in those colonies in the first place finally decided to kick us out.

At the same time, thanks to technology, people had access to all sorts of different modes of travel: cars, motorcycles, trains, buses, helicopters, crop dusters, dinghies, submarines, roller skates, and, of course, bicycles. This meant that they no longer had to live where they worked, as journeys that once took days now took only hours. Forget having a townhouse and a country estate—people could actually work in the city and live in the country, and they didn't even have to be rich to do it. During the day they could be sophisticated burghers, while in the evening they could putter around in their gardens getting all bucolic and cooking meat over an open flame. Suddenly, average schmucks were enjoying a town and country lifestyle that in the Old School days had been the exclusive domain of nobility. We had it pretty good, and we should have been happy.

But we weren't happy. This is because eventually we became the kings and queens of our very own miniature kingdoms, complete with castles (split-level ranches), lavish grounds (well, lawns, and swimming pools), servants (okay, gardeners and paperboys), and of course, a personal fleet of vehicles (sedans, station wagons, minivans, and the rest of it). Consequently, our suburbs became patchworks of fiefdoms, and we became suspicious and insular monarchs and nobles who were fiercely protective of our domains. We also began to wear our self-conferred status on our clothes in the form of designer labels—embroidered polo ponies on our shirts to evoke the country club, other people's initials all over our handbags and leather briefcases, and giant logos on our leisure products as though we were being paid by the companies to endorse them.

But we weren't being paid to endorse these manufacturers and designers. Instead, we were paying to endorse *them*, since the brand names and logos served as the flags we waved over our kingdoms in order to lord over others our wealth and success. And once manufacturers and designers realized just how willing we were to pay to endorse them, they started paying advertising agencies to help move things along. Just as the Old School nobility became patrons of the arts and thus ensured their visages would be rendered in oils for posterity by the great painters of the day, so did the manufacturers and designers engage creative talent to render their images in the form of advertisements and package design. Seduced by this art, we consumed with even more abandon, until the very act of consumption became tantamount to a creative act, and we ourselves became the advertisements, and every single thing we owned had a logo, a spokesperson, and a thirty-second narrative attached to it, right down to our toilet paper.

Moreover, while our circumstances were far cushier, and our linen closets and larders brimming with consumer goods of unprecedented "flambullience," we were still the same miserable people we had been back in Biblical Times. Our DNA was unchanged. In fact, we were even more miserable, since instead of divesting ourselves of all the baggage of history, we just kept carrying it with us each time we entered a new era. Our misery was cumulative—all the wandering, blood-shedding, slave-trading commuters of yore were still sitting on our backs. Moreover, we were loading this cultural baggage and bringing it to and from work with us *every single day*, protected only by a thin veneer of status symbols.

RIGHT ABOUT NOW

Carl Jung talked about the "collective unconscious"—a second psychic system of a collective, universal, and impersonal nature which is identical in all individuals as he explained it—and of archetypal figures that embody our longings, ideals, and beliefs. Similarly, we also share a "collective commuting unconscious," and it is peopled by commuting archetypes such as sinners banished from paradise, crusaders seeking absolution by routing infidels, and subjugating explorers and subjugated natives. The furrows we carve with our travels have become increasingly short and ever more frequent, but they're no less deep, and by Back in the Day, our daily routine had become crushingly mundane, timelessly savage, and thoroughly branded.

This brings us to Right About Now, the period of our history that is occurring, well, right about now. Basically, Right About Now we're living in a Ralph-Naderized version of Back in the Day—the same brutal reality beneath a protective layer of dashboard padding, airbags, and safety restraints. Our streets may feature bike lanes, hidden cameras, traffic-calming devices, and the like, but they're still deadly. And we travel them laden with cultural, historical, spiritual, and emotional baggage that makes us hate each other.

Every day when we set out on our travels, we are expelled from our homes—our Gardens of Eden—and forced to traverse a hostile desert.

Every day as we shout insults and menace each other, we are Crusaders, clashing with others whose beliefs and vehicles are different from ours.

Every day as we break laws and run lights in order to get to work on time, we are imperialists, risking our lives and others' lives so that we can go about the mercenary business of trading and earning.

Every day we carry all of this baggage as we carve the same furrows, back and forth and back and forth, making our way miserably in the Great Wide World.

Sure, it may seem like a bold claim that our commute is essentially a reduction of all of humanity's travels, interactions, and beliefs from the beginning of history until today, but I maintain that it is true. Consider the case of the Hipsters vs. the Hasidim, in which age-old beliefs reached across time to affect modern commuting.

The Tale of the Hipsters vs. the Hasidim

In modern-day Williamsburg, Brooklyn, there are two prominent communities: the Hasidic Jews, who wear black and have beards; and the so-called Hipsters, who wear black and have beards.

In the Hipster community, one of the most favored methods of transportation is the bicycle, while the Hasidim tend to prefer the minivan. Both of them use their respective vehicles on Williamsburg's main drag, Bedford Avenue—except for Saturday, when the Hasidim are forbidden by God to drive their minivans. Hipsters, however, are free to ride their bicycles any day of the week, and the only thing their God prohibits is waking up before 10:30 a.m.

As it happens, Bedford Avenue has a bike lane on it, though this displeased the Hasidim for various reasons. For one thing, they felt the Hipsters who used this bike lane operated their bicycles in a dangerous fashion. For another, anybody who has ever seen Hipsters operate bicycles knows that it involves lots of exposed butt cracks and "muffin tops," and this parade of flesh offended (or possibly aroused—which when you think about it is really the same thing) the pious Hasidim, particularly on their day of rest.

So the Hasidim lobbied the city to remove a portion of the bike lane from their stretch of Bedford Avenue, and that's just what the city did in the winter of 2009.

Among the Hipsters, there was much lamentation and rending of garments (which, once they were rent, the Hipsters sold at exorbitant prices as "fashionably distressed").

"How dare they take our bike lanes!" the Hipsters cried. And so one night, under cover of darkness, they repainted the lanes themselves and recorded it on YouTube, because in the Hipster community recording every single thing you do on YouTube is considered a Hipster *mitzvah* (or, as they call it, a "Meh-tzvah").

The video got many, many views, and at this point the news media began to take notice, because suddenly the two nerdiest groups in all of New York City were having a public slapfight. It was like watching the math club and the chess club rumble in the schoolyard. Also, "Hipsters vs. Hasidim" had a good ring to it, since the media loves alliteration.

Hipsters on track bikes actually told reporters they no longer felt safe without the bike lane, though apparently they felt perfectly safe riding bicycles with no brakes.

In turn, the Hasidim wouldn't go on camera for religious reasons, which only frustrated the Hipsters further. So they retaliated by holding a "funeral procession" (complete with disco dancing clowns), organized by a local advocacy group, in the remnants of the bike lane.

Because if the Hasidim objected to the procession of "coin slots" and muffin tops, why wouldn't they be swayed by disco dancing clowns?

Shockingly, this didn't work either, so a bike messenger organized a naked bike ride just to make sure that any Hasidim who weren't already thoroughly offended were cured of any residual sympathy.

Being winter though, pretty much nobody showed up.

Alas, after this the media wandered away from the slapfight, which had devolved from compelling to pathetic. Arguably, the Hasidim "won," though one might also argue that it was the Hipsters who defeated themselves. In any case, Hipsters can take solace in the fact that any victory that discourages scantily clad people from riding through a neighborhood is a hollow one at best.

So how do we free ourselves from the weight of our commuting history? Most of us can't stop working, nor should any of us become shut-ins, but we also have to stop the commuting madness, and the only way to do that is to drop the baggage. We have to cinch up our pant cuffs, straddle our bicycles, and declare, "I'm dorky as hell, and I'm not going to take it anymore!" But we can't wait for better bike lanes, or safer drivers, or smarter pedestrians, either. We can only effect change in the one thing over which we have total control, which is ourselves. We are the Chosen Commuters after all, and by changing our approach to commuting, we can transform it from misery to joy, and if we cyclists can become joyful commuters, we turn those furrows of frustration into highways of happiness. But first we've got to do a little housecleaning.

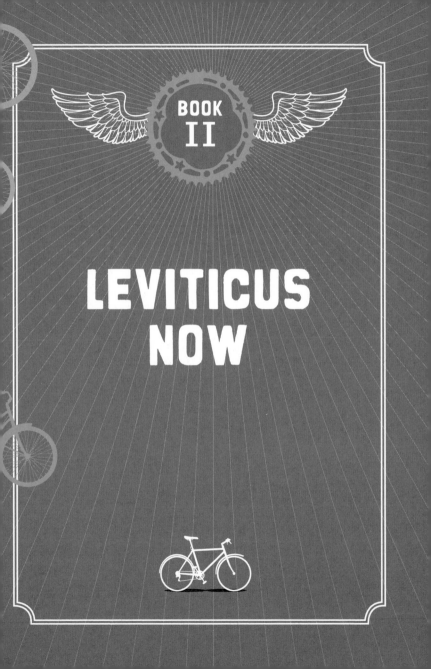

BOOK II

LEVITICUS NOW

ANNOYING CYCLIST BEHAVIOR

If we as a society are going to transcend vehicular prejudice and usher in an age of enlightened commuting bliss, as cyclists we must first look to ourselves and address our own behavior. Once we get our own house in order, we can then move on to the much more enjoyable and rewarding process of telling everybody else what's wrong with them. Following are some of the most common ways in which we cyclists, either wittingly or unwittingly, inconvenience or offend our fellow cyclists.

SALMONING

The salmon is an anadromous fish that is born in fresh water, makes its way to the ocean as a hipster makes its way from the suburbs to Williamsburg, Brooklyn, and then returns to fresh water in order to reproduce, as an aging hipster returns to the suburbs to raise a family. This intriguing fish is famous for two reasons. First, in order to spawn, the salmon makes an "epic" journey against powerful currents, sometimes for well over a hundred miles (also known as a "fish century"). Second, it is delicious, especially on a bagel with cream cheese.

Unfortunately, this beloved fish also has a human cousin that over the years has brought great shame on the noble salmon family: the so-called "bike salmon." Just as the waterborne salmon swims against the current, the bike salmon rides his or her bicycle the wrong way against traffic, a practice colloquially known as "salmoning." Also, while the aquatic salmon's primordial journey is a brave and moving display of the powerful life force that dwells in all living things, the bike salmon's behavior is borne of laziness and is both inconsiderate and reprehensible.

There are few things more irritating than riding along the narrow sliver of pavement between the speeding cars and the sidewalk only to encounter a bike salmon coming toward you. Slipping through

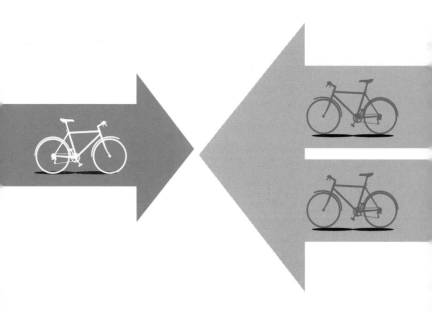

a red light may be sneaky or even foolhardy, but salmoning is just wrong in a way that almost no other form of cycling behavior is, in that the people who do it are literally going about the whole business of cycling in a completely ass-backward fashion. Moreover, it's our job to watch out for them—or so they believe, which is why they'll often ride toward you with total confidence and expect you to simply excuse them like they're moviegoers who need to slip out in the middle of the film in order to use the bathroom.

So what motivates these *Salmonidae velocipedae*? Well, sometimes it's ignorance, very occasionally it's an emergency, but usually it's simply that they can't be bothered to go around the block. However, certain weather-hardened cycling veterans do speak of a bike salmon breeding ground where the salmoners go to spawn. Here, people ride, walk, and even talk backward, and I'll spare you the details about how they engage in coitus, but they do that backward too. (Hint: It involves something called "afterplay.")

While I'm inclined to dismiss this as myth, it could be that's where all these bike salmon are headed, and it would certainly account for that dull, glassy look in their eyes.

SHOALING

In nature, a shoal is a long, narrow strip of land that is formed by the deposits left by ocean currents—basically a sandbar. In cycling, a shoal is what forms at an intersection when cyclists reverse-queue, or "shoal," at red lights. Shoaling does share in common with salmoning the fact that it is essentially backward, but there the similarity ends. While an individual cyclist can shoal you, it takes multiple cyclists to form a true shoal.

Here's how shoaling works: Let's say you're waiting at a red light. Above you is the traffic signal, in front of you is the crosswalk, and beyond is the traffic. Soon, another cyclist arrives. However, instead of stopping behind you, as is the basis of all other line formation in modern Western society, the rider passes you and stops in front of you. Then, *another* cyclist arrives and stops in front of *that* cyclist—and so on. Soon, this formation of wretched humanity extends all the way into the intersection, though it usually veers left or right depending on the direction of perpendicular traffic just like a natural shoal extends into the water and follows the direction of the current. In a densely populated city like New York, a decent-sized shoal consisting of five or six cyclists can form in a matter of seconds. However, like a bunch of pigeons fighting over half a Ring Ding, bicycle shoals are fleeting, and they generally disperse either as soon as there's a big-enough gap in traffic for everybody to run the light or when they are forcibly dispersed by a truck or a city bus.

Even though I detest shoaling, I've often marveled at the shoal itself, in much the same way that I hate getting stung by bees, but find their honeycombs both fascinating and tasty. Watching shoals extend out into the middle of a busy street and curve like a wheat stalk being bent by a prairie wind can be oddly relaxing. Still, the audacity of somebody who feels they can just pull up in front of you and sit there is nearly as maddening as that of the bike salmon. Would you walk in front of somebody waiting to use an ATM?

Would you assume a position at the front of the line when wheeling your shopping cart to the cash register?

Would you sidle up next to someone in a public restroom while they were using the urinal or toilet and attempt to share?

Certainly not—unless of course you're a U.S. Senator.

Then why do it to a fellow cyclist at a red light?

Moreover, unlike some other annoying cycling behaviors, shoaling is not the domain of the reckless or the would-be racer. I have been shoaled by every sort of cyclist you can possibly imagine: parents portaging kids; elderly men; elderly women; and even ladies in sundresses with small dogs in baskets. All of these are the sorts of sweet, wholesome people who would never steal your turn at the ATM or commandeer your urinal, yet they are perfectly comfortable with cutting you off in traffic. Another thing these shoalers have in common is that they're *slow*, which means that most of the time you end up having to go around them anyway as soon as the light turns green. Sometimes though, the faster ones will catch up to you at the next light, at which point they will shoal you again, repeating the maddening cycle. I've watched the same fixed-gear rider shoal me five times in a row, delaying me as he struggled to find his pedals in order to restart every single time. You'd think at a certain point he'd line up behind me, if only to spare himself the embarrassment.

RACING

So much of life depends on context. Take bicycle racing, for example. Sure, bike racing is about riding fast, but it's also much more than that. In its most competitive form, as manifest in races such as the Tour de France, it can be engrossing, thrilling, and even beautiful. The tactics, the high-speed descents, the exquisite suffering on impossibly steep inclines—all of these conspire not only to create a momentous sporting event but also to articulate human nature and our innate desire to transcend suffering, our surroundings, and ourselves.

However, when you move the race from the slopes of the Alpe d'Huez in July to the local bike lane, it is no longer spectacular; instead, it's dork-tastic.

Nevertheless, in the streets and on the bike paths of cities and towns all over America and beyond, cyclists insist on racing their fellow commuters, many of whom are simply going about their business, don't realize they're being raced, and weren't even looking for a race anyway. This is because too many cyclists respond to other cyclists in the same way that a catcalling construction worker responds to an attractive pedestrian: with a hormonal surge that tells him "it's on." As a result, simply riding a bicycle in some places can make you feel like a horse constantly being buzzed by flies, and it can make you wish you had a prehensile tail with a U-lock at the end of it to shoo them away.

Generally speaking, commuter racers (or "Cat 6" racers, or "pathletes"—or, if they attack you on a climb, "Dorko Pantanis") approach their craven art in one of two ways:

The Look

All cycling fans remember "The Look" from the 2001 Tour de France, when Lance Armstrong turned around, looked behind him, and peered menacingly at his arch-rival Jan Ullrich as if to say, "Don't even think about it. I have no intention of folding during the Tour until 2010, when I shall do so spectacularly."

Ever since then, The Look has become a staple of the commuter racer, who will identify an adversary (and by "adversary" I mean "anybody on a bike"), pull ahead of them, and unleash that steely gaze that means only one thing in the world of racing people who don't want to: "Let's have a nerd-tastic commuter-bike slapfight."

When this happens to you, it can be tempting to accept the challenge, if only because you want to wipe The Look right off your challenger's face, but it's almost always better to simply let him (it's usually, though not always, a "him") go. Not only is it more dignified, but you'll also get to laugh when he pulls up on his handlebars too hard, loses his front wheel, and winds up on the pavement.

Wheelsucking

Some unwanted suitors are aggressive, like the "Night at the Roxbury" guys from *Saturday Night Live* (or their predecessors, the "Wild and Crazy Guys"), attacking their quarry with a barrage of cheap pick-up lines. ("You wanna twiddle my spoke nipples?") Others are stalkers, and instead of trying to engage the object of their affection they just follow silently and leer. This is more insidious, and as anybody who's seen *Fatal Attraction* or *Single White Female* knows, far more dangerous.

"Wheelsucking" is a form of nonconsensual drafting that involves sidling up behind somebody unannounced and simply

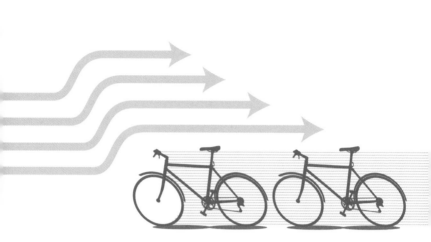

sitting there, and it is the stalking of the cycling world. Different commuter racers have different reasons for drafting: Some want to prove that they can keep up with you, others want a free ride, and still others are simply positioning themselves so that at an opportune moment they can come around you and administer The Look. But whatever the reason, wheelsucking is a very bad idea.

In an actual bike race, riders expect to be drafted; it's a part of the sport, so they ride accordingly. Moreover, they know the people they're riding with have the kind of skill it takes to ride in a tight pack. However, when you're an anonymous wheelsucker, there's no telling what your wheelsuckee might do—for all you know, he or she could be on LSD, which means they're liable to suddenly grab a handful of brake after hallucinating a tie-dyed wildebeest doing that Grateful Dead hippie dance in the middle of the street. Similarly, if you're the wheelsuckee, in the event that something actually does leap into your path (such as an actual tie-dyed wildebeest—I hear that sort of thing sometimes happens in Berkeley) and you are forced into a panic stop, you should not have to also take the anonymous wheelsucker behind you into account. Just as tailgating is unacceptable in a motor vehicle, wheelsucking is unacceptable on a bicycle.

Of course, we all ride for different reasons. Some of us ride for fun, others for fitness, and still others because it's practical. In fact, many of us ride for all three of these reasons. Given this, it's only natural that some people choose to commute more briskly than others—and there's nothing wrong with that, as long as they do so safely, and without wrangling unwitting participants into their role-playing. There's even nothing wrong with using another rider as a sort of pace-setting "mechanical rabbit." However, the difference between doing that and actually racing the person is the violation of space it entails; it's the same as the difference between admiring a stranger from across a crowded subway car and actually making your way over and dry-humping her. Commuter racing is the anonymous dry-humping of the cycling world.

CIRCLING

It's worth noting at this point that much annoying cycling behavior has its analogue in the marine world. There's salmoning, there's shoaling, and there's also "circling." This occurs when, at an intersection, one cyclist rides around and around another, which is a behavior also exhibited by members of the Selachimorpha superorder, colloquially known as "sharks."

The image of a shark's dorsal fin circling an innocent victim is widely believed to herald an impending attack, thanks to movies like *Jaws*, which did for sharks what Long Duk Dong did for Asians in *Sixteen Candles*. In reality, though, sharks circle objects because they are curious about them and because they need to keep moving in order to survive. I'm sure the next time you find yourself circled by a Great White, this knowledge will bring you no comfort whatsoever. The truth is, it's threatening to be circled—especially by creatures with razor-sharp teeth.

Of course, it's foolish to expect that the shark will change its behavior due merely to the fact that humans tend to misinterpret it. First of all, sharks have been doing this since prehistoric times, and old habits are hard to break; and second of all, sharks tend to

grow impatient during etiquette lessons and bite your arms off. Humans on the other hand are considerably more evolved, which makes the fact that they too tend to circle all the more vexing. Simply put, we have much bigger brains than sharks, and we really should know better.

So what compels one rider to circle another at a light? Well, just as the shark must keep swimming, the cyclist must keep cycling in order to live—or at least that's the illusion many cyclists seem to have. This is because few sensations are more pleasant than the seemingly effortless forward motion you experience on a bicycle, and so these cyclists are reluctant to "come down"—the red light is like a nurse threatening to remove us from the morphine drip and wrest us from our narcotic haze. So, instead of simply stopping and waiting, some people instead keep riding in circles—and if you happen to be waiting at the light already, they will ride in circles around you.

The problem, though, is that this is both rude and intimidating. If you were standing on a commuter train platform and a fellow commuter started walking around you in circles, you'd probably avoid eye contact, surreptitiously reach for your cell phone, and pocket-call 911. But what recourse do you have at a red light, when an impatient bicycle commuter is riding around you like some sort of satellite of dorkiness? Like the surfer being circled by a Great White, all you can do is look straight ahead of you, keep the predator in your peripheral vision, and try not to move.

Really, there are only three situations in which circling is socially acceptable:

1. The object you're circling is inanimate, and you are contemplating buying it (e.g., a car or a sofa).

2. You are five years old and you are playing "Duck Duck Goose."

3. You are a tether ball.

If none of these situations apply, then take your place at the back of the line.

Last, it is worth noting that circling has a fixed-gear bicycle analog, which is of course "trackstanding," or the act of balancing on your pedals while remaining stationary. Unlike coasting cyclists, fixed-gear cyclists do not mind stopping, since trackstanding allows them to savor their noncoasting drivetrains and to let other commuters know that they're riding a fixed-gear bicycle and are thus inherently superior. What fixed-gear cyclists *do* mind doing, though, is putting their feet on the pavement, which in the fixed-gear world is a sign of surrender. So they trackstand, and instead of resembling sharks they resemble pointing dogs that have spotted a pheasant in the distance.

Also, for maximum visibility (not for themselves but so others can see them and their bicycles), fixed-gear riders often perform these trackstands at the very tips of shoals.

SUBSTANDARD EQUIPMENT

There is certainly an abundance of snobbery in cycling, and even when it comes to commuting, people tend to put way too much focus on their bicycles and their attire. At the same time, though, it's important to maintain some standards, especially when failing to do so comes at the expense of your fellow cyclists' safety. In the motor vehicular world, mandatory inspections help serve this purpose, but in the world of cycling we must (and should) be self-policing.

Probably the most commonly neglected area of the bicycle is also the most important: the brakes. This neglect takes two forms:

1. **ACTIVE NEGLECT**: Brakeless riding among the "fixerati" is, amazingly, still in fashion. This means the rest of us must look out for the riders who, when their chains fall off their chain rings, have no way to slow their bikes, or whose rear tires finally succumb to that fateful skid and who come barreling out of control down inclines and rolling on bare metal as a result.

2. **PASSIVE NEGLECT**: I have yet to conduct a formal study, but I would estimate that roughly 40 percent of people who ride V-brake-equipped bicycles purely for transportation ride with one or both of these brakes unhooked. This is because most bikes sold in department stores such as Walmart are equipped with V-brakes, and they are assembled with total indifference. Nevertheless, it is a simple matter to attach your V-brakes, and failing to do so is like walking around with your fly open, except for the fact that failing to zip up your pants probably won't result in your getting hit by a car. Sure, department stores don't exactly offer much customer service when they sell you a bike, but ignorance is no excuse. If Walmart customers can figure out how to close their own pants, then they can figure out how to attach their own brakes.

Another extremely common example of substandard equipment is illumination—or, more accurately, the complete lack of it. For some reason, many practical cyclists seem unable or unwilling to affix any sort of light to their bikes, preferring instead to move clumsily and invisibly about in the night, like drunken, clubfooted ninjas. Even more frustrating is that many lightless riders also enjoy engaging in behavior like salmoning, which means they tend to materialize only when it's too late. And perhaps even worse than the rider with no lights is the rider suffering from "light dyslexia," which occurs when the rider uses a red light on the front and/or a white light on the rear, and as a result you have no idea which way they're going. I encounter light-dyslexic bike salmon regularly on my commute, and the effect is disorienting enough to trigger an LSD flashback. It's like watching a mime walk backward on an escalator.

BODILY FLUID MANAGEMENT

When one engages in physical activity, it is important to keep one's breathing passages clear. This is why athletes often engage in lung-purging practices such as "loogie hocking," as well as sinus-expressing methods like the "farmer's blow" or "snot rocket," wherein one expels the contents of one's nose in a burst of mist and mucus.

Unfortunately, too many people perform these acts without making sure there's nobody behind them. Sure, unleashing a snot rocket is an effective and acceptable technique for dispatching with a wheelsucker, but due to the misting factor, it can also inconvenience and nauseate cyclists who are riding behind at a safe and respectful distance. And not only is forcing someone to ride through a cloud of your own mucus disgusting, but it's also unsanitary, and nobody should have to suffer a cold or flu just because some "Cat 6" had to blow his nose.

So if you take nothing else from this chapter, let it be this:

Look before you blow.

FENDING OFF A WHEELSUCKER

Like many commuters, I have fallen victim to wheelsucking more times than I can count. Generally, if I want to dispatch with one, I will simply move aside and slow down, forcing them to pass. Usually this is sufficient, though sometimes it doesn't work and I must actually ask, "Do you mind not sitting on my wheel?" Even then, every once in a long while even that isn't enough, and they insist it is their right to continue violating your personal space. That's when you realize you're dealing with a lunatic and have to resort to desperate measures like dropping thumbtacks behind you or unleashing the oil slick.

Sometimes, however, the unexpected happens.

It was a crisp autumn evening and I was riding home from work along a bike lane in a gentrified neighborhood in Brooklyn when I suddenly became aware of a whooshing sound that seemed to be coming from someplace other than my tires or drivetrain. I looked down at my bicycle to make sure everything was in working order, and it was. That's when I knew that I had either acquired some form of wheelsucker, or else I was being followed by a giant in nylon sweatpants.

Now, for some reason I always refuse to turn around immediately when I suspect wheelsucking is occurring. Instead, I try to pretend it's not happening for awhile, in the same way you'd probably try to pretend the grown man sitting next to you on the airplane isn't having a bizarre psycho-sexual conversation with a Barbie doll. Eventually though, I reconcile myself to the wheelsucker's presence, steel myself, and finally engage in the evasive maneuvers I described above.

This time, however, it was different, because of that whooshing sound. Bicycles don't make whooshing sounds like that, and it was very disconcerting to me. Tentatively, I glanced over one shoulder. I didn't see anything right away, but then, for a brief moment, a hand flew into my peripheral vision. I faced forward again, frightened. What was that?!?

Maybe it *was* a giant in nylon sweatpants! I thought in terror.

Once again I glanced over my shoulder, and the same thing happened—a hand swinging rhythmically in and out of sight. What sort of hideous wheelsucker was this? Finally, I did the old bike racing "steady look under the armpit" thing, and that's when I saw the boots.

I was being wheelsucked by a Rollerblader, and the whooshing was his wheels on the pavement.

I slowed. I speeded up. I pulled off. Nothing could dislodge him. In my panic, I skipped over step two (the "Do you mind not sitting on my wheel?" part) and instead—I'm ashamed to say—lost my temper. I stopped at the next light and angrily told him to stop what he was doing. There might have been an "F" word involved, too, and it wasn't "feet-wheelin'." This confused him, and he couldn't understand how I could possibly object to what he was doing.

"You might crash into me!" I explained. "What if I have to stop?"

"Don't worry," he replied cockily, "I know what I'm doing."

This made me even more angry. Of *course* he thinks he knows what he's doing. That's the definition of being an idiot—thinking you know what you're doing. I know this because I too am an idiot, and I have set all sorts of calamities in motion by thinking I knew what I was doing. I have destroyed bicycle components by turning them the wrong way with tremendous force over several hours. Did I try to turn it the other way? Of course not—I knew I was supposed to turn it this way. The alternative never even crossed my mind.

More important, even if he did know what he was doing, what did that have to do with me? What if someone were to sidle up to you on the subway and start cutting your hair? Imagine telling him to stop and then hearing the reply, "Don't worry, I know what I'm doing." Simply put, no matter how considerable someone's expertise, I should not have to deal with it if I have not engaged it in the first place.

I attempted to convey this with far fewer examples and far more "F" words, and I went on to explain that, while this sort of behavior may be acceptable in the Rollerblading community, it was unacceptable among cyclists.

"No it isn't," he countered. "I do it to cyclists all the time and they never complain."

I was stunned. How was it possible I had not heard tales of this serial Rollerblading wheelsucker? How had I not encountered him before? Most of all, how could nobody complain? Do people actually *like* this? I then moved to conclude the dialogue by telling him he should be more considerate since somebody might be liable to get upset.

"I know how to handle myself," he assured me, puffing up his chest. "I'm from Jersey. I'm from the streets."

I laughed. Sure, New Jersey has some scary streets, but if this guy with the wheeled shoes was from Newark then I was the Sultan of Bahrain.

From there the conversation soon petered out, and we both went our separate ways, but to this day I break into a cold sweat whenever I hear the whooshing of nylon sweatpants.

ANNOYING DRIVER—ON—CYCLIST BEHAVIOR

Being part of a society often involves suspending disbelief and buying into a collective mindset. Consider Lady Gaga—only a populace completely willing to surrender itself to fatuousness could possibly find her or her music interesting. Consider also our own mortality. I mean, regardless of whether we lose our lives in traffic or in bed peacefully at the age of ninety-five, we're all going to die. Guaranteed.

Why, then, do we even bother going about our lives, working and toiling and paying taxes and seeing stupid movies and counting pennies and generally fussing over stuff of little importance? I once saw Steve Winwood in concert for chrissakes (in my defense, it was under duress), and that's like two hours of my life that I will never, ever get back. (I know I will continue to rue that day, even on my deathbed, where I will probably be haunted by the strains of "Roll with It.")

Given this, wouldn't it be healthier to come to terms with our mortality from the outset? Wouldn't we then make better decisions, if only from a time-management perspective? Instead of reading about the exploits of Lady Gaga, we'd spend more time with our loved ones. Instead of seeing Steve Winwood we'd do . . . well, anything. Shouldn't we just start getting this whole mortality thing out of the way in kindergarten, and sing little nursery rhymes about how we're all going to die?

Well, actually, we do—take "Ring Around the Rosie":

Ring around the rosie,
A pocket full of posies,
Ashes! Ashes!
We all fall down!

As it happens, many people say that this seemingly innocuous rhyme is actually a morbid vestige of the Great Plague. Supposedly, the "ring around the rosie" refers to the telltale plague rash, which was a sign of certain death, and the part about the ashes refers to the cremation of the infected bodies.

Fun!

So, really, we do contemplate our mortality—we just do so in a sort of sub-rosa way, and we sublimate it into creepy nursery rhymes, and death metal, and comic books, and other things that let us revel in the inevitability of our demise without having to confront it directly. It's a delicate balance of remembering our time is finite so we don't waste too much of it, but maintaining just enough denial so that we don't stop bothering altogether.

Of course, we don't always get this delicate balance exactly right, and sometimes we get overwhelmed by denial, as is clear from the ways in which we get around. We certainly need cars, but they're also deadly. Almost a half million people in the United States alone have died in cars since the start of the twenty-first century. That's almost the entire population of Portland, Oregon. Just try to imagine the United States without Portland, the sudden loss of beards alone would devastate the personal grooming industry and probably plunge us into another Great Depression.

Given this, it's almost absurd that not only has the car become the dominant form of transportation today, but other ways of getting around—cycling, public transportation, and walking—are considered "alternative transportation." Yes, in most of North America, the act of walking is actually considered "alternative," which would probably come as quite a surprise to your profoundly unhip grandparents.

Imagine meeting a visitor from another time, long before either cars or bicycles roamed the Earth, and explaining to him that you're supposed to wear a helmet on a bike but not in a car.

"So wait, I'm supposed to wear a helmet on that fancy dandy horse, but not in the fast-moving iron death machine?!?"

"Well, yes."

"Why?"

"Uh, to protect you from the cars."

"You mean to say the people in the death machines run into the cyclists, too?"

"Sure, they run into everything."

"Then why not wear a helmet while I'm perambulating on the sidewalk? Has the world gone mad? I must return to my own time and warn the others!"

Indeed, he'd be right, for the world actually has gone mad, and this is all because of our ability to selectively ignore death. So what's the answer? Get rid of cars? Absolutely not, they're very handy. We don't need to take people's cars away, or even restrict access to them.

No, the answer is to get back in touch with the fact that cars are deadly and to drop the denial just as we have to drop our cultural and historical baggage. This can be very difficult in a world in which the car is the default manner of transport, that equates the car with responsibility, practicality, and success, and in which car companies tout only how safe they are, not how deadly they can be.

Most selfishly, we have to remember how to operate a car without killing a cyclist, which is just not that hard to do. Cycling isn't very dangerous as it is, but if drivers could just leave us alone, it would be negligibly dangerous. If you're a cyclist and a driver, you're probably already familiar with the following wrongs. If you're a noncycling driver, here are the behaviors you should abandon.

THE RIGHT HOOK

There's an unspoken rule among drivers, which is that if you see a cyclist, you must get in front of him or her as soon as possible. Apparently, tension and panic mount exponentially with each moment that the driver spends behind the cyclist, and so they either floor the accelerator to pass at the earliest opportunity, or else simply lean on the horn so that the cyclist takes his or her rightful place at the end of the line (or on the sidewalk). And on the rare occasion that a driver is patient enough to wait for an opportune moment to pass, the drivers behind him or her will take up the horn-honking slack (horn-honking being the modern-day equivalent of throwing cabbage and other refuse at someone in a public square, and our culture's predominant way of expressing scorn).

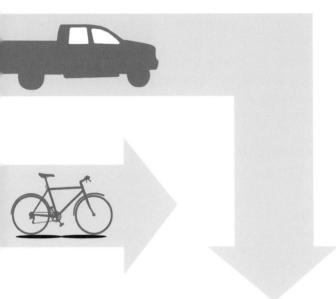

On a straight road, this behavior mostly serves to infuriate the cyclist—especially since, most of the time, once the driver passes, both he and the cyclist wind up at the same red light anyway, rendering the entire dehumanizing maneuver moot. However, when it occurs at an intersection, it often results in an accident and can even be deadly—especially when it comes in the form of the "right hook."

The right hook occurs when a cyclist is going to travel straight through an intersection and the driver behind him is going to make a right turn. Now, in a normal car-on-car situation, the driver behind would never accelerate around the driver in front and then turn—that would be the equivalent of passing somebody on an escalator and then standing still once you reached the top so that the person you just passed wound up dry-humping you. However, if the car ahead of the driver is not a car at all but is instead a hated bicycle, well, let the dry-humping begin. What the driver does in this situation is accelerate, pass, and then turn in front of the cyclist, which naturally results in a collision. And of course, the person who bears all the humiliation and pain resulting from this moronic act of slapstick is the cyclist.

THE WAYWARD DOOR

It's amazing how much serious injury and death we could avoid if only people had learned something from all those *Three Stooges* episodes and *Loony Tunes* cartoons. For example, thanks to these sorts of shows, most people understand that when you fling a door open heedlessly, some unsuspecting person usually sustains a dramatic blow to the face. (This unsuspecting person is also usually carrying a tea tray or similarly fragile item for comic effect.) It's something we grasp even as children. However, for some reason, people seem to forget this right around the time that they get their driver's licenses, since as soon as they get in a car, they start flinging the door open like the interior is filling rapidly with noxious flatulence and they must exit immediately in order to save their own lives.

Of course, just as in the cartoons, when they do this somebody usually smacks right into the door—though it's not a hapless butler. Instead, it's an innocent cyclist.

I guess on a certain level I can understand why some drivers do this. When you're in a car, you're in a very controlled environment—you've got your soundtrack thanks to the stereo, you've got the temperature dialed in thanks to the climate control, and you've got your favorite beverage nestled securely in the cup holder. Then, after navigating your Navigator into that parking space, you gather

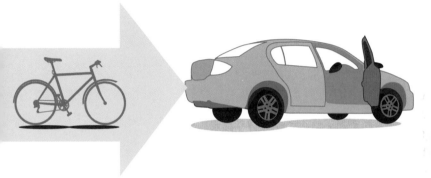

your personal effects—gloves, cell phone, pocketbook—and you leave this environment just as confidently and assuredly as you leave your house in the morning in order to go to work. However, generally speaking you can open your front door just as confidently as you please, since unless your home was suddenly transported by a tornado into the middle of a busy street *Wizard of Oz*–style then chances are there aren't a bunch of people going to and fro right in front of it. At worst, maybe you'll surprise your mail carrier.

But since your car seems like an extension of your home, it's easy to forget that, unlike your home, your car is not a more-or-less permanent feature of the landscape. It is, in fact, a guest in the outside world—and a fairly unwieldy and intrusive one at that. It's the proverbial bull in a china shop, or professional wrestler at a knitting party, or drunkard at a wine tasting. As elegantly appointed and expensive as it may be, in vehicular terms it's a stupid, lumbering oaf.

So take inventory of your surroundings before leaving the car. Dramatic exits are for soap operas and drama queens.

LOAFING, LOITERING, OR OTHERWISE LINGERING

We've all paused briefly in a public space to take care of some personal matter, whether it's tying our shoes, hitching up our pants, or engaging in a time-sensitive cell phone call. The image of the dallying pedestrian is as old as the city itself—a trench-coated PI leaning on a lamppost and lighting a cigarette, a group of people chatting on a stoop on a hot day, and even a homeless person surreptitiously urinating in a phone booth are an integral part of any town's character, charm, and unique aroma.

However, even the most rotund of us is not surrounded by tons of internal combustion engine, sheet metal, and lavishly upholstered seating for up to eight people—unless we're driving our cars, that is. You'd think people would be more considerate when they're dragging all this excess girth, but in practice this is not the case. Sure, it's relatively rare (though not unheard of) to see drivers idling on stoops, but streets, pedestrian crosswalks, and of course bike lanes are all common places where drivers enjoy pausing and supping on their favorite fast-food value meal or engaging in cell phone conversations with

people who aren't important enough to call from home. Sitting in a lavishly expensive automobile and being in people's way is the sort of behavior you might have expected from some turn-of-the-century robber baron, but inexplicably in our modern day, this has become standard practice.

As far as how this affects cyclists, objectively speaking the driver blocking the bike lane is probably one of the more benign driver infractions. Unlike the right hook or the pinball-flipper door, there's plenty of time to avoid the obstacle. However, from a purely symbolic perspective, the bike lane squat is probably the most pro-vocative gesture a driver can make to a cyclist—it's a step short of actually leaving the vehicle and urinating on the bicycle symbol painted on the street. There's just something profoundly infuriating about approaching a motor vehicle in the bike lane and being forced to circumnavigate it, only to see a single person inside cradling a cell phone in the recesses of his or her neck-fat folds and chatting away.

DRIVING DISTRACTED

As a member of the coveted eighteen to sixty-four marketing demographic, I'm old enough to remember a time before cell phones. Indeed, it was a simpler time, and I often reflect fondly on those salad days of the latter portion of the twentieth century. In some ways, for a brief period of time we lived in something of a cultural sweet spot—our TVs were color, our cable stations were many, and we had most of the electronics we have today, but at the same time music videos hadn't yet given way to treacle like *American Idol* and *Glee*, and as a society our cell phones weren't yet dragging us around by our genitals.

Now, as a non-Amish person in the twentieth century who is not a part of the aging and thus noncoveted seventy-five-plus marketing demographic that views things like cell phones and iPads with that quaint, old-people mixture of astonishment, fascination, confusion, and abject fear, I spend as much time pawing my cell phone as members of the postpubescent marketing demographic spend pawing each other and themselves. Furthermore, I have no intention of giving up my cell phone—in fact, you'll have to pry it out of my cold, dead hands. Unfortunately, there's a pretty good chance you *will* have to pry it out of my cold, dead hands, because it's only a matter of time before I get run over by one of these idiots who's always using the phone while driving.

If you've been plying the streets for long enough, you may have noticed the way more and more drivers drift about in bovine oblivion, and if you peer into their windows, you'll notice they're almost always on the phone. Sometimes they're sort of holding the phone with their chins so they look like cats when they do that licking-their-own-chest thing; other times it's in their laps and they're going at it with their fingers like they're simians inspecting their *mons pubis* for lice. But one way or another, the phone is always there, and it's become the root of nearly all driver evil.

Of course, there are laws in many places that prohibit this behavior, but there are also laws against spitting, and when was the last time you saw someone get prosecuted for that (outside of Singapore)? Alas, it may be impossible to rid the world of in-motion cell phone use, and laws banning it may eventually seem as quaint as those old-timey no-spitting statutes. Our only hope may be that technology will come to the rescue, and that brain implants replace cell phones, and we all start communicating via firmware-aided telepathy. In this bold new future, pocket calls will be replaced by accidentally forgetting to disconnect and sharing your most perverse sexual fantasies with everybody on your mental contact list—but at least driving will be that much safer. Maybe.

In the meantime, we can at least make an effort not to do it. If you can refrain from autoerotic stimulation while driving, you can refrain from using your cell phone.

ANNOYING CYCLIST–ON–DRIVER BEHAVIOR

The tragedy inherent in practical cycling is that noncycling drivers hate us, yet we're clearly the victims in the relationship. Cars kill, whereas bicycles mostly just annoy. However, that doesn't mean we don't sometimes treat our oppressors poorly, or that it's right to do so. To really divest ourselves of the baggage of the Collective Commuter Consciousness and become enlightened everyday travelers, we must be compassionate, and of course being truly compassionate is difficult, for there are few things harder than loving your enemy.

Yes, as cyclists, the onus is on us, since as the Chosen Commuters we're one step closer to enlightenment than everybody else. We shouldn't shrug off the idea of cyclist-on-driver abuse in the same way we shouldn't laugh at Lionel Ritchie because his wife beat him up. There's nothing funny about spousal abuse, even when the gender roles are reversed. Plus, the man wrote both "Hello" and "Dancing on the Ceiling," so have some respect. Anyway, sure, drivers may be the Lionel Ritchie in this relationship, but that doesn't mean it's acceptable to treat them poorly.

So just how does a cyclist wrong a driver anyway? Isn't that a near impossibility, like a slave wronging his master, or like the world suddenly being overridden by black rhinos or giant pandas? Not exactly. However, it is extremely difficult for a cyclist to harm a driver in an active way. Lashing out physically while cycling and, say, hitting or kicking a car out of rage is definitely a bad thing to do, but objectively speaking it's not likely to result in much harm. Sure, in our society people tend to take car dents as seriously as knife wounds, but really, in the context of all the human misery and malice I summarized earlier, hitting out at somebody who's safe inside a metal exoskeleton is simply not that bad.

What is bad, however, is what I call "passive assault." This is much worse than yelling or hitting, and it occurs when a cyclist puts a motorist in a position of having not to kill him.

Look, we know there are noncycling motorists out there who hate us, and we even know that some of them are deranged to the point where they may want to harm us. But the vast majority of them are people like us. They want to live, and they want to let live. They want to enjoy delicious foods, and snuggle with adoring pets, and watch entertaining TV shows, and do strange things in private that require them to fabricate elaborate excuses when they go to the doctor after getting something lodged inside of themselves. They don't want to get hurt (well, seriously hurt), nor do they want to hurt others.

In fact, even though people do lash out in fits of rage, and even though we're all the baggage-laden product of generation after generation of cumulative misery, our default mode in an emergency situation is still to act to preserve others. That's why if you're driving a car and somebody suddenly darts out in front of your vehicle on a bicycle after running a red light, you'll stomp on the brakes without even thinking about it. This is because we're programmed not to kill.

However, the problem is that once we've done this, anger often sets in, and this is because we realize something: This person almost made me kill them! Most of us are lucky enough to go through our entire lives without having someone's blood on our hands, and to never have to grapple with the guilt and pain of having seriously harmed or killed somebody. It's about the least savory thing most of us can imagine. So when somebody almost makes us kill them by doing something incredibly stupid—like blowing a light at a very busy intersection—it can make us very, very angry. That light-blowing is "passive assault."

It's possible to passively assault a fellow motorist while you're driving too, but it's much, much easier to passively assault someone in a car while you're riding. In fact, there are entire cycling subcultures based on it—just watch those hill-bombing fixed-gear videos everyone's posting online now and you'll see people passively assaulting motorists all day long. If you're unfamiliar with hill-bombing, it's pretty much what it sounds like—going down a hill really, really fast, and of late, it's become particularly popular to do this on a track bicycle with no brakes. There are few sights more maddening than watching some hipster spinning frantically down a hillside and hurtling directly into traffic in a sublimely moronic act of passive assault, whip-skidding desperately like a running dog trying to gnaw off a dingleberry. If it looks stupid to cyclists, just think of how the noncycling driver interprets it.

As people, we rely on mercy and common sense as our default mode to preserve each other in emergency situations—this is humanity's little built-in insurance policy, and it's really the only reason we haven't totally obliterated ourselves already. However, to take an advance on that mercy by incorporating it into a game, or to use it as a prop in a video in which you're feigning helplessness in the name of style (hill-bombing in a trendy outfit), is to steal goodwill. And when you constantly pilfer little bits of goodwill from others, those little gouges turn into scars of resentment.

It justifies everybody who thinks cyclists are freaks and losers.

PEDESTRIANS: UNDERSTANDING BIPEDAL IDIOCY

Something like four million years ago, the first of our hairy ancestors dispensed with the knuckle-dragging and started walking upright. Moments later, this forward-thinking apeman almost certainly wandered distractedly into a tar pit while gnawing on a drumstick. This was the first pedestrian.

If you commute by bicycle in a crowded city, it can be easy to dismiss pedestrians as the stupidest and least fit for survival of all who ply the streets. They step out suddenly from between parked cars; they dart Frogger-like across busy thoroughfares; they cross wantonly against the light. Sometimes they don't even seem human, they just look like eerily floating coffee cups and cell phones with big clumps of organic matter attached.

Cyclists in particular like to complain about pedestrians. This is because, for all their cluelessness,

pedestrians fear cars and defer to them. However, they tend to look through cyclists like we're insubstantial beings that can't hurt them, like those shape-shifting water creatures in *The Abyss*.

Like squirrels, raccoons, and other forms of potential roadkill, it is true that human pedestrians often appear to have no preservation instincts whatsoever and instead are possessed by what Freud called *thanatos*, the death instinct. As a New Yorker I'm all too familiar with unpredictable pedestrians; I'm sorry to say that I once hit a pedestrian while riding my bicycle to work, though fortunately there were no injuries.

It was one of those pleasant summer mornings that makes you wish you could ride right past your workplace, continue well beyond the city limits, and spend the day either lolling about on the beach or frolicking in the woods with the potential roadkill. I was riding through TriBeCa, which is a downtown neighborhood inhabited by celebrities, and I was approaching Canal Street, where motor vehicles converge and come to a halt as they attempt to funnel themselves into the Holland Tunnel to New Jersey.

Many taxicabs converge here as well, and as I rode, a woman suddenly leaped from the sidewalk in order to obtain one. It was a perfect *Sex and the City*–style cab hail—the designer handbag hanging from the forearm, the cell phone to the ear, the giant celebrity-style sunglasses on the head, and the subtly bejeweled

and beckoning hand raised skyward. The hand was clearly well practiced in the art of summoning people, and it did it as deftly as a fisherman guts his catch. If one were to isolate that hand, one could imagine it attached to any entitled woman in history, and it could just as easily be commanding a sedan chair bearer, or a wine steward, or a handmaiden. It was a gesture that was simultaneously of its place and completely timeless.

Unfortunately, because she was locked into her cycle of dispensing orders to a cabbie with her hand while simultaneously issuing a completely different set of directives over her cell phone to her assistant or domestic or paramour or dogwalker or whoever it was, she did not account for the possibility that other humans not in her employ might actually exist. In particular, she did not think to look before leaping off the sidewalk and directly into my path, and while it was the very last thing I wanted to do, I had no alternative but to hit her.

I sort of hit her with my shoulder, and because she was slight of build she spun elegantly on the toe of her Manolo Blahnik in an impressive pirouette and then collapsed to the pavement amidst her finery like she was concluding a dance of mourning. Naturally I was horrified, and, feeling terrible, I dismounted my bicycle and came to her aid.

"Are you all right?" I asked.

She looked up from gathering her cell phone and regarded me with a withering look of disgust I've only seen a few times in my life. Even the time I stepped right into

somebody's freshly laid cement like it was the Walk of Fame, I did not elicit an expression of this magnitude. Clearly her capacity for belittling people was unharmed, and her reply was something along the lines of:

"What's the matter with you?"

Just as she had pirouetted moments before, so did my concern abruptly turn to anger. I began to explain that she had simply run out into traffic, but by then she had already mentally dismissed me, stood up, and set her sights on the next cab. Indeed, the ability to snub somebody even after being involved in an accident with them is a power possessed only by the most elite members of our society. Satisfied that the incident had reached its mutually disappointng conclusion

and that she had insufficient information with which to sue me, I simply continued on my way.

On a happier note, on another occasion I was able to successfully perform evasive action when Harrison Ford and Calista Flockhart jaywalked into my path, and I'm thankful for that to this day, since I hate to think what a moving bicycle could do to Ms. Flockhart's profoundly diminutive frame.

In any case, as frustrating as pedestrians can be, despite their irritating behavior there are two reasons why we should—indeed we must—indulge them and excuse even the dumbest things they do.

1. An enlightened commuter defers to the more vulnerable party;

And, more important,

2. We're all pedestrians, so if we don't respect our fellow commuters while they're walking, then all is lost.

Think about it: We are animals, and walking is our default mode of transport. It's a basic human function, like sex or going to the bathroom. Sure, like sex and going to the bathroom, people should try to be polite about where and how they do it (for example, you shouldn't walk, have sex, or go to the bathroom on someone's freshly mopped floor), but to deny our age-old right to roam is to deny our very nature.

We're all pedestrians once we step off our bikes and out of our cars. Therefore, we should be sacred when we're on foot, free like cows in India.

Sure, it's annoying that when it comes to walking around town most people are about as careful as squirrels, but at the same time it's kind of comforting. We're animals too, and sometimes we need to roam. In the grand scheme of things, four million years really isn't all that long, and we're still just wandering the plains and finding our legs.

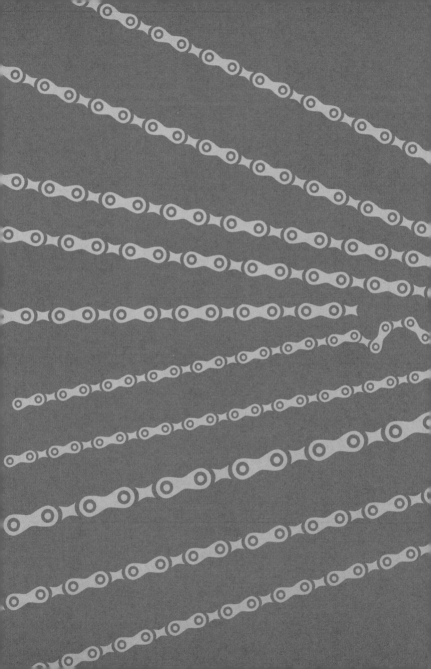

BOOK
III

LET OUR
PEOPLE GO

REVILED:
THE BACKLASH AGAINST CYCLING

Nobody has ever liked cyclists, with the possible exception of other cyclists.

"Shall the Machine Be Allowed in Central Park?" asked an article in the *New York Times* way back on July 15, 1881. "The machine" of course referred to the bicycle and not to a Pink Floyd concert tour (though they certainly seem old enough to have been around at the time). This was long before the bikes vs. cars wars would lay waste to the commuting world. Indeed, it was five years before bicycle repairman Karl Friedrich Benz even patented his "horseless carriage"— which was partially based on the bicycle (Benz was himself a cyclist) and which was probably about as powerful as an apple cart powered by an electric screwdriver at that nascent stage in its development.

No, back then, in the heyday of the pennyfarthing, the bicycle was still the fast-moving bully on the block. Indeed, so threatened were people (or, more accurately, their horses) by these machines that the park commissioners banned them, much to the dismay of bicycle manufacturers and clubs. So an early bicycle lobby challenged the decision, a hearing was held, and as part of the antibicycle testimony one Samuel G. Hough told of the destruction he had seen "the machine" wreak once in Chicago:

Samuel G. Hough, General Manager of the Monarch Line of steam-ships, was the first witness called by Mr. Townsend. He said that he had seen the effect produced upon horses by the bicycle, and that he was prepared to speak very feelingly upon the subject. About two years ago he was driving his team in Chicago, down Wood-street, to reach Washington-street, at which point he proposed to turn. He was driving at the rate of about four miles an hour. His horses were remarkable for their gentleness, and he had driven them past locomotives without their becoming frightened. As he reached Washington-street, which crosses Wood-street at right angles, a bicycle ridden by a man named Glass came from the sidewalk, and without looking to see whether any vehicles were coming down Wood-street, Glass dashed across the street. The bicycle struck one of Mr. Hough's horses, the team gave a start, and then ran away, overturning the buggy and throwing Mr. Hough out.

This in itself is a remarkable find, as Mr. Glass is very possibly the very first sidewalk cyclist in recorded history, and it's certainly no stretch to say that he probably salmoned with abandon as well. Unfortunately, though, we'll never know how this "Salmon Zero" fared after running into a horse on his pennyfarthing, and even worse, we'll never get to see the undoubtedly hilarious video that would have resulted had Thomas Edison been on hand. In fact, all we really know of Mr. Glass is that Mr. Hough's attorneys advised Hough not to sue him because "the man was not worth five cents, and that he rode the bicycle to save his horse-car fare." Cheapskate. However, Mr. Hough was certainly forthcoming about his own injuries:

> *His right arm was broken, as was also the forefinger of his left hand. "I was in the hands of the surgeon for three months," said Mr. Hough, "and during most of that time I was utterly helpless. I had a colored nurse to attend to me, and she had to treat me like an infant, feeding me with a spoon. My buggy was smashed to pieces, and one of my horses died."*

Remember, this was Back in the Day, and one can imagine a late nineteenth-century gentleman and successful steamship manager with a team of horses like Mr. Hough had little patience for people of color and poor people who couldn't afford horse-car fare, but his harshest words were reserved for the bicycle itself:

> *I consider the bicycle to be the most dangerous thing to life ever invented. The gentlest of horses are afraid of it.*

Obviously, in the ensuing years, many things would change. Pennyfarthings would give way to the safety bicycle. Overt racial prejudice would yield to the more subtle, veiled variety. Pink Floyd would record the first-ever phonograph record, produced by Thomas Edison. And of course, the bicycle would soon cede its position as the scariest wheeled vehicle plying the streets to the automobile, a machine possessing the power of hundreds of horses and able to terrorize and dominate even the most reckless cyclist.

Glass and his high-wheeler may have scared the manure out of Hough's mighty team of horses, but he would have been no match for a single elderly lady in a Buick.

Nevertheless, people's attitudes toward the bicycle have not changed. Today bicycles are allowed in Central Park—as are cars, by the way, but only during rush hour—and the horses that pull tourists around and around it endlessly in sad Sisyphean fashion got used to all of them long ago. (The only way to scare a Central Park horse is to wave a bottle of glue at him.) People, however, are apparently not nearly as adaptable as the equine. In 2009, motor vehicles killed 256 people in New York City alone (amazingly this was an improvement over previous years), whereas bicycles killed nobody and frightened exactly no horses. Still, most people seem to be fine with cars—even though they're private, we seem to have accepted them as a part of the infrastructure, like trains and buses—but the general public still hates bicycles, and it hates cyclists.

Why? What's the problem?

Well, the problem isn't really that bicycles are menacing, as Mr. Hough said. It's that they're annoying. There's an idea floating around that people on bicycles simply do whatever they want. That's why Mr. Hough hated them, that's why the old lady in the Buick hates them, that's why pedestrians hate them, and that's why people say stuff like this:

- "I swear to you," ESPN radio host Tony Kornheiser famously said of cyclists in March of 2010, "it's all you can do to not run them down! Why do these people think that these roads were built for bicycles?"

- "Lob something at their heads," advised the hosts of the Deminski and Doyle radio show in Detroit the year before.
- "I wish people would hit them, just clip them and send them flying over their handlebars," said a DJ in Birmingham, Alabama, that same year.

"So what?" you may be asking yourself. "Didn't terrestrial radio go out with black and white television and rabbit ears? Who cares about a bunch of losers imitating early Howard Stern while missing the point?" Well, sure, but the yammering of these people is the white noise of irritation that permeates our society, and we ignore it at our peril. Morning radio shows are like those vending machines full of fake tattoos and hip-hop jewelry you find at supermarket checkouts and highway rest areas—it's total garbage, but as cultural detritus it still says a lot about the society that produces and consumes it.

More to the point, unlike TV and the Internet, this is the stuff people are consuming when they're actually in their cars, simmering because they're sitting in traffic on the way to a job they don't like. Now, I'm as much of a free speech fan as any other God-indifferent American, but it is disconcerting nonetheless. It takes only a tiny bit of pressure on an accelerator pedal to cut off that annoying cyclist who has the temerity to dart effortlessly through the morass in which you're stuck, and that little irritated twitch of the loafer can be the difference between life and death. Going on the radio and telling people to "run them down" is like goading somebody while he's cleaning his gun.

The radio is far from the only place society articulates its disdain for bicycles and the people who ride them. It's also present in more "refined" forms of entertainment, such as film and TV, where cyclists are generally represented in one of four ways: the hapless wussbag, the homoerotic fitness dork, the self-important, tree-humping, enviro-douche Luddite, or the freakish man-child.

The Hapless Wussbag

Let's say you're making a movie about a gigantic, middle-aged nerd who collects action figures and is still a virgin. What mode of transport would your protagonist employ?

An SUV or a sports sedan? Certainly not—those are for successful people who are rich in money and coitus.

Well, then how about an environmentally sensitive hybrid car, like a Prius? Yeah, sure, they are appropriately diminutive, but they're also expensive, and thus are subtle status symbols—and status is something our protagonist doesn't have.

What about a motorcycle? No, motorcyclists are rebels who live life on their own terms, like Peter Fonda and Dennis Hopper in *Easy Rider* or Matthew McConaughey in that movie where he's a womanizing douchebag. (Which I guess is every Matthew McConaughey movie, but there was one in particular where he had a Triumph Bonneville and lived on Staten Island of all places.)

OK, then—a Vespa. Surely no self-respecting male adult would ride one of those. Well, yeah—except suave Italians like Marcello Mastroianni, or those 1960s mods. No, come to think of it, not even the lowly Vespa is neutered enough.

Ah—of course! He'd ride a bicycle! Obviously, this was indeed the case with Steve Carell's character in *The 40-Year-Old Virgin*. Hey, I liked the movie too, but as the film proves, there's no better way to make an adult seem nonthreatening and ineffectual than to place him atop a bicycle. It's instant pathos! Indeed, what could be more

emasculating than getting around on a machine that doesn't have an engine, and what could be more humiliating than telling a woman that you don't drive?

The Homoerotic Fitness Dork

I was watching the show *Californication* a while back, and if you're one of those smug people who likes to brag about not having a TV, *Californication* is that one where David Duchovny plays a lascivious, hedonistic writer with a heart of gold. He also drives a beat-up Porsche, which symbolizes his reckless libido and his wild nature, as well as his downfall from literary wunderkind to washed-up cad.

Also, people get naked.

Anyway, in this particular episode, Duchovny is driving along in his rolling plot device when he comes upon one of the most absurdly Fred-tastic parodies of a road cyclist I've ever seen, complete with teardrop time-trial helmet and what appears to be a Rock Racing jersey. (The Fred is played by Peter Gallagher with both of his preternaturally bushy eyebrows in supporting roles.)

Naturally, like most American drivers, Duchovny's character is disgusted by the fact that he has to slow for this guy, and so he lays on the horn. An argument naturally ensues, and Duchovny's character finally says, "Live Strong, asshole," and flicks his cigarette into Gallagher's face.

Amazingly, Gallagher's eyebrows do not burst into flames, but he does crash into some shrubbery (or, more likely, a stunt double with some pipe cleaner glued to his forehead crashes into some shrubbery) and we're all supposed to laugh at the self-importance of the clown-like cyclist, as well as the irreverence of Duchovny's character—who, after all, does all of the things we wish we could do, like

drink in the morning, smoke cigarettes indoors, have vast quantities of sex, and of course, send those stupid cyclists flying headlong into shrubbery.

Characters like Gallagher's also appear randomly in movie chase scenes, where they're used like fruit stands and chickens in that their purpose is to scatter comically when the car comes barreling across the screen.

The Self-Important, Tree-Humping, Enviro-Douche Luddite

If cyclists aren't self-importantly bettering themselves physically and rubbing our noses in it like Peter Gallagher's character, then they're saving the Earth and reminding everyone else what evil fossil fuel–burning, rain forest–devouring juggernauts they are. And if there's one thing people like to be reminded of less than how unhealthy they are, it's how irresponsible and inconsiderate they are.

Of course, there is plenty of smugness in the cycling world, but the truth is that only a small number of people who ride bikes are *that* smug, and to say that they feel superior to other people is true only in the most general and simplistic sense. As for the rest of us, we don't have time to worry about how much gasoline other people are burning, and plenty of us live in oil-heated homes or run through the occasional tank of high octane ourselves. Still, when you're on a bike, you're only one thing to drivers—a cyclist—and the mere sight of you can be enough to tickle their deep-seated feelings of inadequacy and insecurity. They think you're telling them there's something wrong with them.

A comedian named Tom Segura recently articulated this attitude perfectly. Sure, stand-up comedy is not what it once was, and with the exception of people like Louis C.K. and Chris Rock, stand-up comedians are arguably only half a notch above morning radio DJs in terms of cultural import, but in this case Segura sums up this aspect of the way people perceive cyclists so neatly that it's worth exploring. First, he begins with a disclaimer: "I think if you ride a bike, that's healthy and that's green and now you should shut up and get on the sidewalk."

Notice that he has to make the disclaimer wherein he acknowledges that it's healthy and green, as if that were the only point of cycling. Mostly these are just fringe benefits, and we ride because it's practical, yet bicycle-haters consider those things unassailable and instead attack the thing that should be inalienable, which is the cyclist's right to the road. It's always, "I know it's healthy and green but . . . ," and this is because they're insecure—it's like asking someone for a date and saying, "I know you're attractive and I'm ugly but . . ." It immediately reduces everything to superficialities and all but ensures that any subsequent interactions will fail.

Anyway, he goes on to express his general disgust with the cyclist who has the temerity to ride in the street and not on the sidewalk, and then he asks: "Don't you see me in my car? The thing that will rupture your spleen if I tap you with it?"

This elicits much laughter and applause.

I know this is supposed to be "comedy," and he's certainly "joking." I've also laughed at far worse humor (I once saw Andrew "Dice" Clay live back in the '80s), and I do my best not to be that guy who can't laugh when the joke is on him. At the same time, people really do feel this way, and when you think about it, that's really scary—not only do they find cyclists so irritating that they burst into laughter at the thought of rupturing their spleens, but they actually do rupture their spleens. If Segura were doing a routine about working in a kitchen and in his mock exchange he said to the guy washing the lettuce, "Don't you see me chopping meat with my cleaver? The thing that will chop off your fingers if I attack you with it?" then the bit wouldn't work. Who really hates lettuce? "Sure, lettuce is healthy and green and all that, but I'm working with meat here. One flick of the knife and I've taken off your fingers!" Nobody would laugh—they'd probably smile politely and think he was psychotic. But say it about cyclists, and you get big laughs.

His conclusion though is the best part: "Why are you riding a bike? This is the age of technology. This isn't Ho Chi Minh City in 1976. Get a hundred bucks a month together and lease a Honda, and if you can't do that maybe you should move—to Ho Chi Minh City."

I know I listened to too many Dead Kennedys records as a kid (to this day when I hear a cat yowling in heat my first thought is, "Is that you, Jello?"), but it's odd to me that anyone would equate paying a bank on a monthly basis to borrow a car for a few years as some sign of achievement—as though success means being in thrall to a bank, an automobile manufacturer, and an insurance company all at the same time. Are we that far gone as a culture that the stereotype of the "working stiff" has become the ideal to which people aspire? There's not even pride of ownership involved in this scenario—the lessee will most likely never even open the hood of his own vehicle, will take no responsibility for its maintenance, and will indeed never even look upon the motor that powers it. He will look at a cyclist and hate him though, honking the horn and maybe even revving the mysterious thing under the hood that magically propels his borrowed vehicle forward.

And as far as a car representing the "age of technology," bicycles and cars were invented at almost the same time. Sure, the bicycle is technically a little bit older than the automobile, but it's not like it's some piece of flint from the Paleolithic age and the automobile is a laser. Plus, while the automobile is certainly the clear winner for long trips or truly big hauls, in terms of commuting and practical local travel, it's cumbersome and primitive, expensive and unwieldy, and completely unable to match the bicycle in terms of efficiency, maneuverability, and operating costs. Saying that you should drive instead of ride because this is the "age of technology" is like saying you should send messages not by cell phone or computer but instead by pasting them onto laser-guided missiles and firing them at the recipient because that's somehow more sophisticated.

The Freakish Man-Child

Obviously *Pee-wee's Big Adventure* (easily one of my favorite films) is the *Citizen Kane* of freakish man-child movies, but it's certainly worth noting that the embodiment of his strangely suppressed id is his wildly festooned bicycle. Of course, if we're to be totally fair, while Pee-wee and his ride are both rather surreal, in terms of their relationship, the movie pretty much nails it—plenty of cyclists do polish their bicycles obsessively and even talk to them. This is not unique to cycling, and people do this with their cars, and their motorcycles, and their golf clubs, too—that's just human nature. Really, as a culture, the only thing we seem to have trouble loving and tending to is each other.

Still, cyclists do bear the brunt of the "freak" stereotype—though it's not entirely unwarranted, since we are kind of the nerds in the school cafeteria of transportation, and after a while it's inevitable we should start sitting together and dorking out.

Nevertheless, even if our popular entertainment doesn't reflect it yet, regular nonfreak, nonself-important, and nonhapless people really are commuting by bicycle—more people than ever, in fact, and the numbers continue to increase every year. Governments are noticing this, too. Not only are many cities adding bicycle infrastructure to accommodate these bicycle commuters, but even the federal government has acknowledged the need. In 2010, Transportation Secretary Ray LaHood announced a "major policy revision" that stated, "Walking and biking should not be an afterthought in roadway design."

On the surface of it, this would seem to be a good thing, and you'd think that everybody would be happy. Cyclists would have their own place on the road, drivers would have to interact with them less, and—crazy as it may sound—people might even have an easier time walking places. Unfortunately, this hasn't been the case, and instead drivers are getting even more angry. Why?

Because cyclists are annoying, and they do whatever they want.

To better understand this, consider the noncyclist's mindset. People who are not ambivehicular lack object permanence. When they see a person on a bike, they don't see a fellow person who happens to be riding a bike. Instead, they see a strange person-bike entity that is permanently fused, kind of like a centaur. For some reason, it's impossible to imagine that this person actually gets off his bike when he gets someplace, or that he might also get into and out of a car, or that he may even go to a job and do work. They also don't realize that this work generates income, which results in taxes for the government, which goes in part to building and maintaining roads. Many people are under the mistaken impression that only their gas money pays for the roads, but that's not true—it's the income tax we all pay. Therefore, the noncyclist sees the weird cycle centaur and thinks it's this freakish being that flits hither and thither, sustaining itself on motion and smugness, and that it gives nothing back in return.

On top of this, they can't tell one of these person-bike centaurs from another, or differentiate between a recreational cyclist and a cyclist who's riding for practical purposes. You might be riding to work, but the noncycling driver thinks you're playing a game. In their minds, they might as well be building an infrastructure for Rollerbladers.

"We're building bike lanes for these?!?" exclaims the noncyclist, as though it were tantamount to using public funds to build a park for unicorns or a retirement home for elderly Hobbits.

Meanwhile, for their part, many cyclists don't really know how to use the infrastructure they're getting either—which is not entirely their fault. Ten years ago, as far as a lot of people were concerned, you were supposed to ride your bike on the sidewalk until you were old enough to drive, and then you were supposed to ditch the whole enterprise. Now, not only are you supposed to share the road with cars, but you're also supposed to obey the exact same laws, act like you've got the same degree of protection, and be fluent in a vocabulary of hand signals that ranks in complexity somewhere between American sign language and semaphore code.

So, if everybody hates cyclists so much, why did they even start building bike lanes in the first place? Sure, more people may be riding, but bicycles have been all over the place since the late nineteenth century, so why start this now? Well, because cycling is "healthy and green," of course. Just like Tom Segura has to acknowledge this before he tells cyclists to move to Ho Chi Minh City, I'm sure plenty of people in plenty of cities liked the idea of a bicycle network until they actually got one—that's certainly been the case in my hometown of New York. "Oh, yeah, bikes—very healthy, very green," I'm sure people said in the beginning when they started reading newspaper articles about it. But then the lanes actually started appearing and that primordial hatred from back in the days of Mr. Hough and his agitated horses returned. "Wait, *bikes*? On the *streets*? What the hell was I thinking?!?"

As incongruous as it seems, every so often a coyote wanders into Manhattan. This isn't really that surprising, since like anything else that lives in Jersey all it has to do is wander over the George Washington bridge. However, unlike Carmine from Hackensack, a coyote can't just hang out in Manhattan. Even though they were here long before there was a Carmine, or a Hackensack, or really anything constructed, and even though we encroached on the coyotes' habitat long before they encroached on ours, as soon as they show their fuzzy little snouts, they get loaded with tranquilizer darts and sent to animal control.

Sure, this makes sense, since the coyote may be dangerous, but arguably the same thing could be said about Carmine.

In this sense, cyclists are like coyotes. While we don't predate Hackensack (or even the subway, really), we have been here longer than cars. Arguably, the entire car-centric transportation infrastructure has encroached on us, not the other way around. Yet, everyone still sees us as the dangerous and unpredictable coyotes, and given the way people see cyclists, it would not surprise me to one day feel the sting of a tranquilizer in my rump.

Of course, while people are very uncomfortable sharing the streets with coyotes, they're more than comfortable sharing their sidewalks and their homes and even their meals with the coyote's sycophantic cousin, the domesticated dog—provided of course that the dog is duly licensed and vaccinated, and preferably also neutered and perhaps even a holder of some sort of pedigree.

Similarly, the latest proposition politicians in various cities have been putting forward is the idea of licensing cyclists and registering bicycles in an attempt to "domesticate" us, the rationale being that this would mitigate that horse-frightening tendency we have to launch ourselves off of sidewalks unannounced and force people into the care of colored nurses. Recently, New York City Councilman Eric Ulrich proposed such a law in New York City using the following argument:

> I have never, never seen a cop car pull over a bicyclist for running through a red light. I wish they would, because those are the ones who are creating problems every day in the city. If these people are not obeying traffic laws, they should be held accountable.

Of course, just because he hasn't seen a bicyclist get a ticket doesn't mean it doesn't happen all the time—it does. Moreover, at least in New York City, the schedule of fines for traffic infractions on a bicycle is the same as for a car. This is yet another example of the object permanence problem, and just as noncyclists see people on bikes as strange centaur creatures, they also can't imagine them getting tickets for the sole reason that they've never seen it. I very rarely see squirrels have sex either, but the damn things are all over the place, so at a certain point I have to take it for granted that they are in fact "getting down." Yes, squirrels *do* get tail, and cyclists *do* get tickets. It's as simple as that.

To me, what really seems to be at the heart of the whole bicycle registration thing is the fact that owning and operating a car is a major pain in the ass—as it should be. A car is a powerful machine, the biggest one most of us will ever use in our lives, so naturally you need a license to operate it, an inspection sticker to make sure your wheels don't fall off and your hood doesn't pop open when you're doing 60 mph on the Interstate, a registration sticker so the government can hold you accountable when you drive into your neighbor's patio, and an insurance policy to cover you for the damage to their deluxe gas grill.

Given this, it can be very frustrating to the noncycling driver when he or she looks through his or her government-stickered windshield and sees some shirtless guy on a beach cruiser blowing a light while smoking a joint with one of those '70s-style roach clips with all the feathers hanging off it. "Why should I have to go through all this crap when he doesn't?" they think. And they certainly do have a point.

Still, there's no getting around the fact that a bicycle is not a car, nor is it capable of wreaking nearly as much havoc as a car is. As far as the infrastructure goes, you're an afterthought, but when it comes to punishment, you're equal.

This is the biggest paradox of all—the way in which we simultaneously seem unable to accord human beings an equal level of respect when they're riding bicycles, yet at the same time are determined to subject them to the same laws and requirements that apply to them if they are driving. We're an odd bunch in that way. Consider the airport, for example, where we take great pains to subject everybody to the same amount of scrutiny and dismemberment as they pass through security, and where the shifty-eyed and the wheelchair-bound senior are picked apart to an equal degree. Could a nonambulatory great-grandmother in fact be an agent of some insidious terrorist group? Sure. Is it likely? No. Similarly, could a stoned guy on a beach cruiser run down and kill somebody? Sure. Is it likely? Not really—he's more likely to spill a smoothie on them.

Nevertheless, we seem to want to treat our shared streets like the airport and make sure that everybody's equally miserable to maintain the illusion of safety, even if it comes at the expense of actual safety. We'd probably be safer if different people were subjected to different levels of scrutiny at the airport, just as we'd probably be safer if the roads accommodated different users differently. Instead, the way it works here if you ride a bicycle is this:

Strap on that helmet and pretend you're a car.

So here we are, well over a century and a quarter after this Glass guy terrorized those horses, and almost nothing has changed. In this sense, there's not so much a bicycle backlash as there is an almost constant disapproval of them punctuated by brief moments of flirtation with legitimacy and tolerance.

THE GREAT NEW YORK CITY BICYCLE CRACKDOWN OF 2011

During the first decade of the twenty-first century, New York City began a new love affair with the bicycle. Mayor Michael Bloomberg and Commissioner of the New York City Department of Transportation Janette Sadik-Khan set about improving the quality of life in New York City, and an unprecedented expansion of the bike lane network was an integral part of this. "Mmmm, yes. Bike lanes. Healthy, green," people murmured to each other in the way they do about things they're supposed to like. Bicycle commuting increased significantly. People, it seemed, were happy.

But then something started to happen. It turned out some people weren't happy, and that they didn't like the bike lanes or the people who used them. At the same time, even though the city was doing all these good things for cyclists, they continued to engage in massive Critical Mass rides. Soon there was a backlash—against the mayor, the commissioner, and ultimately the cyclists—which eventually became a full-scale crackdown on pretty much anybody on a bike. Here's a somewhat subjective but nevertheless telling timeline of the major events which precipitated it and created the current climate:

JANUARY 2002 | Michael Bloomberg becomes mayor. Among his priorities is "PlaNYC," a vision to improve

the cleanliness, safety, and livability of the city over a twenty-five year period. An improved cycling infrastructure is an integral part of this.

2003 | The Williamsburg Bridge renovations are completed. For the first time you can ride over it without actually seeing the water below you. This further encourages newly arrived hipsters to take to their bicycles. Some of them commute, others reinvent themselves as fixed-gear renegades and still others as '60s-style radicals by participating in Critical Mass.

2004–2006 | Critical Mass becomes swollen with newly arrived hipsters. The police arrest various Critical Mass participants for minor traffic infractions.

MARCH 2007 | A local bicycle club files a lawsuit in federal court to stop a new NYPD rule. Designed to thwart Critical Mass, it requires any group of fifty or more cyclists riding together to first obtain a parade permit.

APRIL 2007 | Michael Bloomberg appoints Janet Sadik-Khan to replace Iris Weinshall as the commissioner of the New York City Department of Transportation. She sets about implementing bike lanes, pedestrian plazas, and other features with tremendous momentum and full mayoral support.

OCTOBER 2007 | A bunch of those wrongfully arrested Critical Mass cyclists file a lawsuit against the city.

MARCH 2008 | Senator Charles Schumer (husband of Iris Weinshall) writes a whimsical piece in the Five Boro Bike Tour program about how he likes to ride his bike from Park Slope to Rockaway. (I am published in the same program, and so is David Byrne.)

JULY 2008 | Rookie NYPD officer Patrick Pogan bodychecks a Critical Mass participant by the name of Christopher Long. The incident is captured on amateur video and becomes a YouTube sensation.

NOVEMBER–DECEMBER 2009 | The city removes a portion of the Bedford Avenue bike lane at the behest of the local Hasidim. Enraged hipsters do actual manual labor repaint it. The repainting becomes a YouTube sensation.

FEBRUARY 2010 | The federal judge upholds the legality of the parade rule.

APRIL 2010 | NYPD bodychecker Patrick Pogan is found guilty for filing a false criminal complaint against Christopher Long, but is found not guilty for misdemeanor assault, even though everybody saw him do it thanks to the fact that the amateur video of it had become a YouTube sensation.

JUNE 2010 | The city begins installing a luxurious lime green protected bike lane on Prospect Park West along Brooklyn's Prospect Park.

OCTOBER 2010 | The city settles with the Critical Mass participants for $965,000.

OCTOBER 2010 | A small group of Park Slopers protests the new Prospect Park West bike lane, claiming it is somehow dangerous to senior citizens.

JANUARY 2011 | NYPD announces a bicycle traffic violation crackdown and ticket blitz. Suddenly regular, non–Critical Mass, non-fixed-gear renegades are getting tickets for things like not having bells on their bikes and not wearing helmets (even though there's no law requiring adults to wear helmets). Local cyclists begin complaining of harassment.

FEBRUARY 2011 | The NYPD begins aggressively ticketing cyclists for riding through red lights, even during car-free hours.

FEBRUARY 2011 | Despite community support and the fact that the Prospect Park West bike lane is demonstrably safer, a group of well-connected Park Slopers organize themselves as the "Neighbors for Better Bike Lanes" and sue the city to remove it. (Iris Weinshall is among the group's supporters, and Schumer himself is conspicuously silent.)

MARCH 2011 | A *New York Times* profile of Janet Sadik-Khan articulates criticism of her methods; aspiring mayor Anthony Wiener tells the paper, "When I become mayor, you know what I'm going to spend my first year doing? I'm going to have a bunch of ribbon-cuttings tearing out your [expletive] bike lanes."

MARCH 2011 | Police set up a speed trap in Central Park and ticket cyclists for riding faster than 15 mph. When it turns out no such speed-limit law exists, the police must visit the riders' homes and apologize.

APRIL 2011 | The city sends out eighty-three Critical Mass settlement checks, which the recipients presumably squander on brand-new bamboo bicycles and organic vegetables from their local food co-ops.

APRIL 2011 | A woman on a bicycle is almost doored by an undercover cop, who proceeds to arrest her.

APRIL 2011 | A woman is ticketed for hanging a tote bag on her handlebars.

MAY 2011 | Bike Month NYC 2011 begins, and the Department of Transportation celebrates by announcing its new "Don't Be a Jerk" campaign, in which it tells cyclists to stop being jerks.

TO MARKET, TO MARKET:
HOW CYCLING IS SOLD

Sure, lots of people hate cycling. But that doesn't mean there ain't money in it.

Earlier on, I looked at the Bible. As I mentioned, according to this popular work of fiction (the biggest bestseller of all time after the Harry Potter books), the first humans were a couple named Adam and Eve, who God made more or less instantly, in the same manner you might prepare a pair of Pop Tarts. They lived in the Garden of Eden, which made them essentially the first gentrifiers on Earth. Like any gentrified hipsters, Adam and Eve were bohemian types, and they walked around their bountiful proto-Williamsburg in a state of nudity and smugness.

Naturally, though, it wasn't long before a wily serpentine salesman identified these naïve young hipsters as the world's very first marketing demographic. And if there's one thing hipsters can't

resist, it's a clever marketing campaign. "Eat this piece of fruit," said the serpent. "It's organically grown and totally sustainable." Five minutes later, Adam and Eve experienced those first pangs of self-consciousness, and soon they were spending their entire paychecks at the local Edenic Apparel in order to buy stylish clothing opaque enough to conceal their genitals yet snug enough to remind each other that their genitals were still there.

Today, little has changed, and ever since that fateful moment of conspicuous consumerism, we have been unable to engage in even the simplest activity without constructing some sort of identity around it and purchasing a bunch of equipment and accessories before even attempting it. This is especially true of riding bicycles—in fact, it's so true that even Web sites for those "naked bike rides" that pop up all over the place usually include FAQs. If you need to peruse an FAQ in order to figure out how to ride your bike naked, then you may be overthinking things.

That Tree of Knowledge fruit was some powerful stuff.

Of course, the degree to which people overthink everyday cycling can be inverse to how common everyday cycling is in a particular location. For example, in places like Copenhagen and Amsterdam, people seem able to straddle nearly identical bicycles while wearing street clothes and go about their business. In most of America, on the other hand, only the very Zen (I mean actually Zen, not the fixed-gear version of Zen) and the very poor seem able to do that. Everybody else seems to need some sort of lugged artisanal pedigree "townie" bike and a pair of two-hundred-dollar "technical pants," or else a stylized race bike and some designer-ified messenger gear, before they're ready to face the simple task of riding a bicycle from one place to the other in a noncompetitive fashion.

This is hardly surprising, and to a certain extent you really can't blame people for this sort of behavior. Despite being the most common mode of transportation in the world (apart from walking), the bicycle is viewed as marginal in many places, and therefore sometimes you need to have an above-average level of passion for the bicycle and for cycling in order to transcend the stigma and inconvenience imposed upon you by your local "society" in order to ride one. And naturally, when I say "passion," I of course mean "geekiness." We are freakish man-children (or women-children) after all, and bikes attract geeks like muscle cars attract hairy-chested medallion enthusiasts. There are many ways to define what it means to be a geek, but certainly one definition has to be, "Someone who does something normal people do, only while wearing special pants and talking about it constantly."

So, being in the middle of a "bike boom" at the moment, we find ourselves approaching a major cultural intersection: Will cycling finally go mainstream?

Indeed, this is the moment of truth. Right now, the light at this intersection is a flashing yellow, and one of two things is going to happen: Either that light's going to turn green and cycling will finally be considered normal and unremarkable, or it will go back to red again and we'll return to being perceived as a bunch of geeky scofflaws, making our way through the cracks of an infrastructure specially designed not to accommodate us.

But why now? Why, to paraphrase the Haggadah, is this "bike boom" different from all other bike booms? Certainly "geeking out" over bicycles is nothing new—they are ideal machines for the mechanically ambitious to fawn over and customize. Furthermore, bike booms are also nothing new. When the pennyfarthing came out, it was the hottest lopsided vehicle since the riding kangaroo. Then, when the "safety bicycle" arrived, everyone wanted those and sold their old "p-fars" on whatever the equivalent of Craigslist was at the time to retrogrouches with giant handlebar moustaches. Years later, when Greg LeMond won the Tour de France, everyone wanted road racing bikes; and when mountain bikes came out, everyone wanted mountain bikes, which they rode on the street for a couple of weeks before consigning them to those suburban bicycle tombs known as garages. After that, when Lance Armstrong won the Tour de France, everyone wanted road bikes again, even though they never did end up riding their mountain bikes and they already had perfectly good Greg LeMond–era road bikes sitting in the garage beneath a thin layer of dust.

Well, the difference is that, unlike the aforementioned booms, which were mostly based on recreational cycling, this one is actually based on practical cycling.

Sure, "practical" is relative, since one major component of this particular bike boom is the urban track bike, which is about as practical as using a whippet as a pack mule, but still, much of what's so popular at the moment is simply using a bicycle to get around. Everywhere, young people are returning home to the suburbs for the weekend from whichever city they're in the process of gentrifying, removing those mountain bikes and LeMond-era road bikes from their parents' garages, bringing them back into the city, and actually riding them simply in order to get places. They may be doing horrific things to those bikes, like putting Aerospokes and DayGlo tires on them, but they are riding them nonetheless, and arguably that's a better use of them than a life of quiet moldering punctuated by occasional charity rides beneath the half-shorted crotch of a negligent owner wearing a helmet mirror and a Primal jersey.

But if we learned anything from the Garden of Eden story, it's two things:

1. Never trust a talking snake.
2. People can't resist marketing.

And, like Adam and Eve, as soon as you're more than one person, you're a marketing demographic. This means our nascent practicality-minded bike boom is already being seduced by an array of bicycles, accessories, and potential identities so vast that before you can even pull on the second leg of your snug-fitting boutique technical pants, the first leg has already gone out of style.

So what's so wrong with that? Nobody's forcing us to buy this stuff, right? Plus, it's nice to have options. And isn't it a good sign for the future of cycling for transportation that there's a demand for this stuff in the first place? Absolutely yes . . . ish. All of that stuff represents the Good Part. The Bad Part, though, is that when you throw too much fuel onto a fire, you run the risk of extinguishing it. There also used to be some good bands in Seattle, and I shouldn't have to remind you what happened when Nirvana got popular—before long they started giving away Sub Pop recording contracts free with the purchase of a flannel shirt, then the whole thing went national, then Kurt Cobain killed himself, and it finally reached its hideous, sickening apotheosis with the advent of the band Creed.

Similarly, when practical cycling becomes too focused on gear, it runs the risk of becoming like all other forms of cycling—strange, inscrutable, niche activities for borderline fetishists. Now, don't get me wrong—I'm one of these borderline fetishists myself, and I delight in encasing myself sausage-like in Lycra so that I may ride both recreationally and competitively. However, I also delight in running errands on a piece of crap while dressed like a schlub, and it's this more than any other form of cycling from which the population at large stands to gain the most. When it comes to practical cycling, there should be no barriers to entry, because the moment a person asks, "Do I really need the technical pants?" and some total bike geek with a nylon U-lock holster and a carabiner full of keys who looks like he's about to climb a telephone pole and repair the power lines answers, "Yes," the whole deal is off.

All these bike lanes are no good if we need to wear a costume to use them.

In any case, sure, some decent bikey stuff can certainly come in handy, but like anything else it's important to keep that in perspective. In order to do so, it's a good idea to have a handle on how practical cycling is marketed, so you can cherry-pick from the various offerings or even ignore it altogether when you're confronted with it.

TYPES OF BICYCLES

You might think that it would be much easier to purchase a practical bicycle than a racing bicycle. All a practical bike has to do is take you and your stuff from one place to another without falling apart, while a racing bicycle must make use of cutting-edge technology in order to perform as well as possible for the competitive rider. This is not the case. Remember, we're talking about cycling here, and the simpler it gets, the more people need to complicate it.

The truth is, purchasing a racing bicycle is easy, mostly because racing bikes have to adhere to standards set forth by the governing body of whatever discipline you're competing in. All you do is pick a light frame, buy a drivetrain from one of only three companies who make them, add some decent wheels, and you're done. Sure, people obsess over it, but at a certain point the hardened racer learns that it's mostly the same stuff with different decals.

Practical bicycles on the other hand are another story, since there's no commuting equivalent of the Union Cycliste Internationale—there's just your local police force, which probably alternately ignores you and harasses you. This means that various companies, hand builders, and independent entrepreneurs all compete to sell you their interpretation of what they think you should be riding. Here's what's popular at the moment.

The American Urban Commuting Bike

When you're commuting, two things are likely:

1. You're going to encounter crappy weather.
2. You're going to need to carry stuff.

It would follow then that the urban commuting bike would include provisions for things like fenders and racks. Naturally, then, the current iteration of the urban commuting bike often takes neither of these things into account, inasmuch as it is modeled on a racing bike. Moreover, it's not just modeled on any racing bike—it's modeled on a *track* racing bike, which is designed to be used indoors by people wearing skinsuits. If there's a form of cycling more antithetical to bicycle commuting than this, I have yet to see it.

So why are these types of bicycles so popular with commuters at the moment? Well, some people will tell you that they're "minimalist," but this isn't true at all. In fact, they're exactly the opposite, because what happens is that all the provisions that would ordinarily be included on the bike instead migrate to the rider's body, which results in a whole other level of purchasing that often costs more than the bicycle itself. For example, since the bicycle has no provisions for racks, the rider instead must employ some sort of bag, usually of the designer cycling variety, and often in conjunction with some sort of holster or fanny-pack-like belt arrangement. And since there are no fenders to deflect moisture and grit, the rider's wardrobe must repel it yet look like ordinary street clothes—hence the two-hundred-dollar technical pants and other assorted garments. The result is a thousand dollars in clothing and luggage that essentially serves the same purpose as about fifty dollars in baskets and fenders. And even then it's not enough, since inevitably laundry day arrives. Even the most committed schlub can't wear the same clothes *every* day. Fenders, on the other hand, never require changing.

Dutch Bikes

So what do you do if these repurposed racing bikes aren't for you? Well, increasingly, many American urbanites are turning to Dutch-style bicycles and other European-style commuters. Unlike the American Urban Commuting Bike, which was born in the velodrome, the Dutch-style bike is actually designed so that the average trench-coat-wearing, briefcase-toting office worker can straddle it as easily and unthinkingly as an Amsterdam red-light-district sex worker straddles a stoned tourist with a money belt full of traveler's checks.

However, what is utilitarian in one country is a luxury item in another. If you're old enough to remember the 1980s, you may remember those tales of Russians paying a hundred dollars for cheap bits of Americana like Levis blue jeans. (This was before Levi realized it could also get away with charging Americans the same price—

in fact that's probably how they figured it out.) Similarly, the Dutch bike, which in Amsterdam is alternately ridden, neglected, stolen by junkies, thrown into canals, and then dredged out of them so that the cycle of life can begin anew, is the latest urban status symbol here in cosmopolitan American cities, a staple in photo spreads and boutique windows, and can command prices well over a thousand dollars.

Taking into account the inherent practicality and durability of the Dutch bicycle, it would stand to reason that the owner would eventually amortize the considerable cost—until you realize that the other problem with the Dutch bike is that it is large, heavy, and unwieldy, and is designed to be left outdoors. This works well in Amsterdam, where there is outdoor bicycle parking, but not so well in some American cities like New York, where theft is rampant and where many people must keep their bicycles inside their apartments. It's one thing if you live in a converted loft space with a freight elevator, but it's quite another if you live in a fourth-floor walk-up, in which case carrying your portly Dutch bike up the stairs is an endeavor akin to bringing home a drunken wrestler.

Sure, you could just leave it outside like the Dutch do, but don't forget it cost you a thousand dollars, and like any bike, odds are it will be stolen, removed by the police or an irritable landlord, or simply mangled by a garbage truck or inept parallel parker in relatively short order. So while the Dutch bike may embody simple cycling, in much of America it is more of a hopeful symbol of simple cycling, and in practice the cost is a large chunk of change and, very possibly, a hernia.

Cargo Bikes

Do you live in a city? If so, do you have a garage? Of course you don't—you keep your bike in your apartment. That's why you don't have a Dutch bike, right? Well, clear out even more of that imaginary space you don't have, because the hot new thing is the cargo bike.

Cargo bikes come in many forms, but among the smug the most desirable is the so-called *Bakfiets* (or "bake feets" as I call them) which is—you guessed it—of Dutch origin and basically looks like a wheelbarrow with wheels. The way it works is you throw whatever cargo you have into the wheelbarrow part—your groceries, your kids, your shrine to Al Gore—and you transport them hither and thither under your own power in a cumbersome yet majestic display of self-satisfaction. In New York City these have become something of a smug status symbol, and I've been salmoned by riders carrying as many as three nonplussed children in them.

Like its more nimble cousin the Dutch bike, the *Bakfiets* is about as well suited to most North American environments as the SUV is to places like Amsterdam and Copenhagen (not like SUVs are well suited to American cities either). Now, this is not to impugn cargo bikes in general, which are great in that they enable you to carry all sorts of stuff without having to purchase and carry designer cycling bags or strap bulky items precariously to the racks of bicycles with relatively short wheelbases (so long as you have a place to store it, naturally). In fact, I'm surprised bike-hating societies have been so loath to embrace the cargo bike since it doesn't inhibit our lifestyle of mindless consumerism. Let's say you're on your way home from work and you pass a store that's having a sale on something you really shouldn't buy but is simply too cheap to pass up, like an entire shipping pallet of Froot Loops cereal for $5.99. On a regular bike, you'll be forced to pass it up, whereas on a cargo bike (as in a car) you'll figure, "Well, why not? I've got the room," and by the end of the week you'll have eaten so many bowls of sugar and food coloring that you'll be hallucinating toucans. Come to think of it, this may be why our culture is so against bicycles—overdoing it is the American way, so maybe enough "epic" cargo-bike Walmart or Costco hauls might be enough to turn the tide.

Folding Bikes

The folding bicycle is the cargo bike's tiny, collapsible cousin. These would seem to be an obvious choice for the typical city-dweller, inasmuch as you could probably fit as many as twenty folding bicycles in a single "bake feets."

More important, you don't have to leave a folding bike outside. It's astonishing how expensive some of the bicycles people lock up

outside are—you might as well chain up a top-of-the-line laptop. If somebody decides they want your bike, one way or another they're going to get it, and a folding bicycle obviously obviates this concern. Plus, you can take it on the train or the bus, and tailor your commuting experience.

The trade-off is that, depending on your size, you may look like a performing circus bear when you ride it.

A folding bicycle can also help you sidestep our society's strict antibicycle rules, since bicycles are welcome in even fewer establishments than cigarette smokers and dogs. However, I have heard tales from folding bicycle owners of airlines charging them extra despite the diminutive size and of public transit systems prohibiting them. Apparently a bicycle has the same power to offend no matter how small it is.

THE IMAGES

The bike you choose is very important, partially because you need to ride the thing, but mostly because it needs to complement the cycling image you've chosen for yourself. One recent favorite that never fails to get press is "Cycle Chic."

Cycle Chic and Various Permutations Thereof

Cycle Chic is, first and foremost, about looking "fabulous" in a way that suggests you don't ride a bike at all. Here are just a few things that the Cycle Chic like to wear:

- Scarves
- Skirts
- High-heeled shoes
- Dainty loafers
- Leather gloves
- Tweed (see "Tweed Rides," page 150)
- Cable-knit sweaters

Basically, the idea is to look like Dick Cavett or Anna Wintour, depending on your gender. Newspapers like the *New York Times* will publish an article about Cycle Chic at least twice a season, and about how these people like to ride bikes without making a fuss about it, whereas it's immediately obvious that they make a huge fuss about everything.

There are various Web sites devoted to the aesthetic, like Copenhagen Cycle Chic, which is a strangely voyeuristic site that marries advocacy with photographs taken of attractive women's pantylines on the streets of Denmark as they ride. There's also The Sartorialist, which is more a general fashion site, but which includes a lot of Cycle

Chic types, most of whom dress and pose like old-timey airplane pilots and look like they should be in biplanes instead of on bicycles.

Amazingly, many advocates of Cycle Chic are not only completely unaware of how absurd they look, but they also think they make other people want to ride bikes. Somehow they think this makes the whole enterprise "accessible," which is kind of like the captain of a stunningly expensive yacht thinking he makes boating look accessible.

The Urban Look

The counterpart to Cycle Chic is the urban look. Because the track-inspired urban bicycle has few provisions for accessories, all of these accessories have migrated onto the rider—backpacks, hip pouches, U-lock holsters, tool rolls, and utility belts are the order of the day. Consequently, urban cyclists tend to look as though they're about to rappel down a cliff face or hook up your cable TV for you.

Cycling baggage in particular has reached the point at which it is becoming bewildering, with companies now offering bags in every conceivable configuration with more pockets than a kangaroo orgy. This is because urban cyclists have to carry every piece of bicycle-related equipment they own at all times—because anything can happen on that half-mile ride to the bar. And to feed this paranoia, urban cycling companies continue to introduce new tools and accessories, all of which have integrated bottle openers on them, since it's apparently illegal to design a bicycle accessory that doesn't double as a bottle opener. Unfortunately, while urban cyclists do love their little accessories and gadgets, they also get very uncomfortable if they don't have a special dedicated compartment for every single one of them. (Yet strangely these very same people are perfectly fine with letting their house keys hang from their pants by a carabiner.)

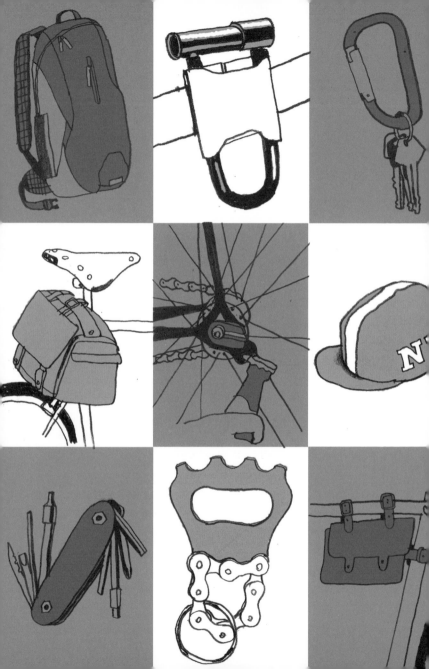

"Where am I supposed to put this?!?" cries the urban cyclist as he studies his new integrated headset press/lockring remover/chain tool/Brooks saddle chamfering knife/bottle opener. "I'm going to need a new bag!"

Therefore, every time a new tool or accessory comes out, a bag company has to design a new bag that includes a special pocket for that tool or accessory, and they're getting far more complicated than the ostensibly simple fixed-gear bicycles they're supposed to complement.

The result of all of this is a frenzy of tool-and-bag manufacturing that is spiraling wildly out of control, and will end only when some urban cycling company perfects a one-piece wearable bag bodysuit ensemble, or else these people simply begin dying under the weight of all their stuff.

THE HOLIDAYS

Holidays serve an important function in our society, in that they allow us to take time out to appreciate or commemorate a group of people, a historical event, or a certain aspect of the human spirit so that we can feel good about ourselves and then forget about it for the rest of the year. This allows us to compartmentalize our sense of responsibility. On Memorial Day, we pretend to keep our soldiers in the back of our mind while we barbecue. On Presidents' Day, we honor George Washington and Abraham Lincoln by incorporating their visages into advertisements for sales and by enjoying big, big savings. And on New Year's Day, we resolve to become better people— at least until our hangovers wear off.

Naturally, cycling has its own holiday too, which is called "Bike Month." Bike Month takes place in May, and it's strategically positioned at a point on the calendar during which most places in North America are experiencing pleasant weather, yet people are still feeling the aftereffects of winter-induced cabin fever and are willing to try just about anything—including riding bicycles to work in a transportation infrastructure that either neglects cyclists or is actively hostile to them, depending on your particular locale.

Bike Month celebrations also vary from city to city, but the festivities usually culminate in some sort of "Bike to Work Day," or even a "Bike to Work Week" if the local populace is not so out of shape that an entire week's worth of cycling is likely to kill them. (Decimating an entire city or town would not be good for cycling's ostensibly healthy image.) During that time, legions of people excavate disused and neglected bicycles from their garages or basements, violate pretty much every single traffic law and bit of bicycle etiquette out of complete ignorance, and then congratulate themselves for doing something healthy for themselves and the Earth, until one of the following happens:

- Bike to Work [insert time period here] ends.
- They are nearly killed by a car.
- June arrives, they decide it's too hot to ride a bike, and they retreat to the climate-controlled cabins of their Volkswagen Jettas.

Really, the surest way to make certain the rest of the year is *not* bike friendly is to have a Bike Month, since it operates on the same principle as the "all you can eat" buffet. Restaurant owners know that bingeing is their friend in that even the most gluttonous customer can eat only so much food before becoming totally stuffed. The same goes for Bike Month, after which most people are more than ready to return to their cars like an overstuffed customer finally hitting the restroom. Instead of having Bike to Work Day, they should have *Drive* to Work Day; the resulting traffic jams would probably do more to encourage people to explore other forms of transit. Hunger begets appreciation; gorging begets nausea.

"HEY GUYS, CAN I PLAY TOO?" TYPES OF NONCOMPETITIVE GROUP RIDES

Is the anonymity of commuting getting you down? Do you seek the companionship of other cyclists in a (theoretically) noncompetitive environment? Well, there are all sorts of rides out there, and depending on where you live, you can partake in some or all of them—just as long as you don't mind sacrificing all your dignity and possibly getting arrested. Here are just a few.

CHARITY RIDES

Charity rides are just what they sound like: organized rides that raise money and awareness for a cause. AIDS, MS, and cancer are just a few of the illnesses participants ride to combat.

PROS: They are well-organized, there are frequent rest areas, and they are legal.

CONS: You're just as likely to be crashed by a would-be racer on a custom Serotta as you are by a second-time cyclist on a beach cruiser or a fleet of recumbents.

TWEED RIDES

Increasingly in cities all over the world, cyclists are discovering the joys of riding around together while dressed like contemporaries of Jules Verne.

PROS: You get to wear affectations such as bloomers, knickers, and knee socks, if that sort of thing interests you. Plus, if you bring a penny-farthing you'll become an instant Flickr celebrity.

CONS: Ever seen what tweed can do to an inner thigh on a summer day?

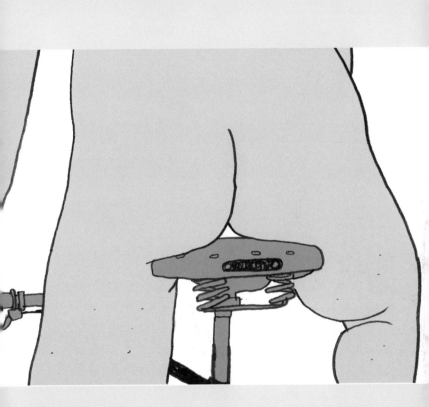

NAKED RIDES

Like a tweed ride, only with no clothing whatsoever.

PROS: Naked cyclists.

CONS: Naked cyclists. Ever seen a naked inner thigh that has been exposed to tweed on a summer day?

CRITICAL MASS RIDES

This is the "bad boy," the *Fight Club* of noncompetitive group rides—except instead of hitting people you just radiate smugness at one another. Ostensibly, Critical Mass is a worldwide movement with no leader in which cyclists meet organically on the last Friday of every month and assert their rights to the road by snarling traffic. In terms of the "bike culture," this is a mild gateway drug to the sordid world of alleycat racing or mutant tall-bike jousting gangs.

PROS: You get to feel like a real-life civil rights activist, and you'll probably reconnect with half your graduating class at Bard, Oberlin, Wesleyan, or Sara Lawrence.

CONS: You might *really* get to feel like a real-life civil rights activist when you get arrested.

BIKES VS. CARS:
WHAT ARE WE FIGHTING FOR?

Cars aren't going anywhere.

I don't mean that they're not *moving*. Sure, they do spend a lot of time idling in traffic, but they're definitely moving—all over the place, from city to city, state to state, country to country, and often into pedestrians, cyclists, and each other.

No, what I mean is that cars aren't going away. For all the problems associated with them, if you grab even the most smug environmentalist by the collar of his hemp shirt, back him up against the wall of his composting toilet, get all up in his bearded face, and threaten to ask for plastic bags instead of paper next time you go shopping at Whole Foods, he will admit that the hated car is an incredibly useful invention. Even people who don't have them don't *casually* not have them; instead, they constantly make a very big point of not having them in the same way that people who profess to hate celebrities seem unable to ignore them. Or, maybe they subscribe to "car-sharing" programs, which allow them to drive without having to cop to car ownership, and which is kind of like saying you're a vegetarian even though you take bites from your friend's hamburger. In this sense cars are a lot like cell phones—they're irritating appliances that bring out the worst in us, yet still we're unable to live without them. The only difference is that it's pretty hard to kill a person with a cell phone alone, unless you can throw it with deadly accuracy like Naomi Campbell (though in conjunction with a car they're nothing short of astonishing death wands—you'd think iPhones came with a "drive and kill" app preloaded).

Given this, some of the more smug cyclists live in eternal hope that humanity will somehow realize the error of its ways and reject the automobile altogether, and that we'll return to some sort of bucolic idyll that never was, in which ladies and gentlemen smile and wave at each other as they move across a rolling green landscape completely under their own power.

This is not going to happen.

Sure, that would be much "nicer," but never in the history of the world has humanity forfeited an invention that makes our lives profoundly easier, as the car does. Nobody ever said, "This newsprint is making my fingers filthy. I'm going back to smoke signals." TV was supposed to rot your brain and ruin your eyes, but instead of going away it only got bigger and flatter, and we now have like four hundred channels instead of three. And airplanes are still the world's preferred mode of very-long-distance travel, even though terrorists still try to fly them into buildings and we now have to be dismantled into our component atoms, sifted through, and reassembled in order to board them. So if we have yet to jettison these abominations, why would people give up their cars either?

Of course, none of this is to say that the car is inherently superior, or to imply that the bicycle is going to go away or be *supplanted* by the car. This is emphatically not the case, and indeed the bicycle is even less likely to go away than the car. First of all, the bicycle is older than the car (not by much, but it is older) and it's still here. Second of all, there's an aphorism regarding bicycle components that goes something like: "Light, strong, cheap—pick any two." That may be true relatively speaking, and it's the reason that those carbon-spoked Mavic wheels tended to explode, but when it comes to the bicycle itself, the machine is in fact light *and* strong *and* cheap, none of which can be said about a car. In fact, if you're halfway savvy, you can probably pick up a serviceable used bike for about the price of a tank of gas (though admittedly you'll have to wallow in the hell that is Craigslist in order to get it). There will always be a demand for the sort of inexpensive, efficient, and accessible transportation the bicycle represents. A car is great when you're traveling hundreds of miles on the highway with Van Halen's "Panama" on the stereo and your bare feet out the window, but anybody who's driven a car in the city and dealt with heavy traffic and scarce parking has inevitably experienced that frustrating moment of desperation when you ask yourself, "What the hell am I going to do with this thing?" It feels like someone asked you to watch their St. Bernard while they ran into the store and then never came back.

In other words, cars are for the broad strokes, while bikes are for the detail work. The well-rounded modern individual uses both of them in a complementary fashion, and in proportion to their geography and relative needs.

Still, for some reason, we seem unable to conceive of a world in which people seamlessly move from one form of transportation to another depending on where we're going and what we're doing—and, more important, of a world in which people don't shout "Cocksucker!" at each other. Instead, our culture seems to want us to pledge our allegiance to one vehicle over another. This is why we're constantly inundated with fatuous news stories about the so-called "Bikes vs. Cars" debate. Just plug that phrase into the Internet search engine of your choice and you'll find thousands of articles on the subject, followed by hundreds of thousands of angry comments from readers telling each other to get off the road.

In our culture, you're not just a person. Instead, you are what you drive (or ride). Never mind that what you're driving or riding might change on a daily or even hourly basis. That's too complicated. You're supposed to pledge your undying loyalty to one or the other.

The truth is, debating the legitimacy of bikes vs. cars is about as stupid an argument as it is possible to have—it's like debating microwave ovens vs. barbecue grills. Some people use one or the other, some people use neither, and some people use both. And sure, both cook food, but nobody is going to assume that if you own one you're somehow opposed to the other. This is because most of us are smart enough to understand that when you're heating up last night's leftovers, you're not going to fire up the Weber, and that when you're inviting some friends over to eat and drink beer outside, you're not going to wheel your microwave out onto the patio, strap on your "Kiss the Cook" apron, and serve Hungry-Man Salisbury steaks (unless of course you want to lose all your friends, or you're an extremely ironic hipster).

But when it comes to integrating our transportation, we're as closed-minded as the racists of yesteryear. For most of us today the notion that, say, white people and black people shouldn't be allowed to get married is so old-fashioned that it is no longer deeply offensive so much as it is simply quaint and laughable—the kind of thing a senile nonagenarian might say as he accidentally microwaves (or barbecues) his false teeth. But tell most people that you ride a bike, and they'll automatically assume you hate all cars. And write a *book* about riding bikes, and they'll think you're some kind of zealot. After my book *Bike Snob* was published (available from Chronicle Books at a bookseller near you; it makes a great holiday gift and/or light bathroom reading; buy three), radio interviewers would routinely ask me questions like, "Why do you hate cars?" Once a photographer even suggested I wear a shirt that said "Fuck Cars" to a shoot. Why is it so hard for them to imagine that a cyclist can like something without hating something else? Nobody ever asks professional baseball players why they hate hockey so much, and I bet nobody ever told the Dog Whisperer to wear a shirt that said "Fuck Cats."

I know what you're saying: "There's an important difference. Drivers run down cyclists all the time, but César Millán has never sicced a German shepherd on a Siamese." This is true. However, this does not mean that "Bikes vs. Cars" is a legitimate debate. Actually, it's a smokescreen—an easy way for politicians and the media to get people angry at each other. Once you wave away the smoke, it becomes obvious that the two vehicles are complementary, and the only reasonable argument is for their complete integration.

Let's look at the typical cyclist. Unless he or she is one of those ultraconservative types who refuses to have any interaction whatsoever with the hated motor vehicle, he or she probably utilizes one from time to time. Maybe it's taking a taxi to the airport or renting a car when visiting a place where things are spread out and transportation is scarce. Maybe it's embarking on a road trip with family and friends. Or, maybe it's *actually owning a car*. Yes, believe it or not, many cyclists also own cars. Owning both a bike and a car is not some sort of cosmic paradox that will cause the universe to collapse on itself. Trust me, Yakima and Thule would not be selling so many roof racks if people weren't using bikes and cars together. Where do people think those racks go anyway, on horses? (Amish craftsmen would no doubt corner the equine bike-rack market anyway.)

Moreover, in addition to the car, the typical cyclist (being a citizen of the modern world, after all) also utilizes many other types of transportation depending on circumstances, including trains, buses, boats, airplanes, and at times even his or her own feet.

If you step off a plane at the airport, will a reporter ask you why you hate cars? Or trains? Or bikes for that matter? If you step out of a car, is someone there asking you why you hate all other kinds of transportation? No. But thanks to this whole bikes vs. cars thing, if you interview that very same cyclist about cycling, he or she will be forced to account for him- or herself, and to answer that same annoying question:

"Why do you hate cars so much?"

So where is this all this coming from, anyway? Yes, it's a smokescreen, but how does the smoke machine work to begin with? Sure, bikes vs. cars is a media construct to a large extent, thanks mostly to the fact that it inspires the indignant commentary and "flame wars" that fuel blogs and the flickering electronic ghosts of the deceased media entities once known as "newspapers." And sure, it's also partly due to the sorts of cyclists I mentioned earlier who do think the motor vehicle is inherently evil and refuse to acknowledge its legitimacy. But mostly, like any wrongheaded and counterproductive notion, it's fueled mostly by simple ignorance. Consider, for example, the sorts of people who *never* ride bikes.

Now, there's nothing's wrong with this—some people have never operated a boat either. But there's a difference between never using something because you have no use for it and not understanding that other people do have a use for it. Unfortunately, this is what happens with some people who drive but never ride bikes—they have no use for bikes, and therefore they conclude that bikes are useless and that they somehow don't "belong." It's like someone who lives in the desert deciding that boats should be banned.

Furthermore, when these people do see a person on a bike, they get irritated because they don't really understand what they're seeing. In one of those radio interviews during which I was being forced to account for myself as a cyclist, a caller wanted me to commiserate with him about the fact that, when driving, he sometimes encounters cyclists. Then (horror of horrors) he sometimes has to *slow down* before he can safely pass them. He didn't seem to have any "solution" for this supposed "problem." Rather, he mostly just wanted me to feel his pain, and I suppose offer some sort of acknowledgment of guilt.

As it happens, the audience for this particular radio show was roughly in the middle of nowhere, and I knew this because, unbeknownst to the caller who probably assumed I'd never left "the big city," I had indeed visited and in fact driven in the exact nowhere from which he was calling. Consequently, I knew that such maddening occurrences as "traffic jams" really do not occur there (unless a logging truck jackknifes, I suppose), and that what he was objecting to was simply, on occasion, having to brush his brake pedal lightly with his shoe and then turn his steering wheel a couple of degrees while en route to his destination. I have no idea why this would even qualify as an inconvenience, unless over a period of a few years it is causing him slightly uneven tire wear.

As I listened to his heartfelt complaint about having to execute what was an almost immeasurable series of physical motions, it occurred to me that I had just stumbled on the cause of the entire bikes vs. cars debate. It isn't the murderous drivers, or the lawless cyclists, or the carnage on the roads. It is the millions of people everywhere behind the wheels of motor vehicles who are simply vexed by the sight of people riding bicycles even though they're not being inconvenienced by them, and the various media outlets who pander to and justify their irritation.

This simultaneously troubled and relieved me. On one hand, I was glad to finally realize that all of this is really no more serious than people not liking other people's ringtones. On the other hand, similarly innocuous issues have resulted in actual wars and genocides. It's like having a Christina Aguilera ringtone and stabbing someone because their phone plays Britney Spears.

Because many people view cyclists as little more than an inconvenience, the cyclist occupies an odd place in our culture, and consequently experiences "Double Commuter Consciousness."

The great intellectual W.E.B. Du Bois used to say that black people in America had what he called a "double consciousness"—a uniquely complex self-image because, as Americans, they could not help but see themselves in part through the eyes of prejudiced white Americans. As he explains it in *The Souls of Black Folk*:

> *It is a peculiar sensation, this double consciousness, this sense of always looking at one's self through the eyes of others, of measuring one's soul by the tape of a world that looks on in amused contempt and pity. One ever feels his two-ness,— an American, a Negro; two warring souls, two thoughts, two unreconciled strivings; two warring ideals in one dark body, whose dogged strength alone keeps it from being torn asunder.*

Cyclists, too, experience "double consciousness" when it comes to getting around. Raised in a society in which cars are the norm, we're well aware that many drivers see us as any one (or more) of the following:

- Rolling inconveniences who use the roads without paying enough,
- Irritatingly smug "wussy" liberal eco-warriors who may or may not be homosexuals,
- Overgrown children who belong on the sidewalk,
- Adrenaline junkie bike messengers with esoteric body piercings who sleep on bare mattresses and live in loft apartments without heat and with lots of roommates,
- Some variation on the old "Spandex-clad Lance Armstrong wannabe" slur.

All cyclists have encountered these generalizations, either in the media or while riding, or from the relative or coworker who doesn't realize you ride a bike because you're not clad in Spandex at that moment. Naturally then, as Du Bois said, these stereotypes become part of the cyclist's self-image, and his or her behavior can sometimes be informed by them in any number of ways, including the following:

- "Everybody expects me to run the light, so I might as well do it."
- "These laws were made to protect drivers and not me, nobody cares whether I live or die, so I might as well run the light."
- "I will seek the acceptance of an alternative culture by wearing a dirty cycling cap, riding a fixed-gear bicycle, and piercing esoteric body parts."

None of these, incidentally, precludes car ownership, for even the most avowedly anticar person can usually come up with some rationale for that motor vehicle in the driveway. (Usually some variation on, "It was a birthday/wedding/graduation gift from my parents and if I were to sell it or give it away it could fall into the wrong hands.") It's just that if you ride a marginalized form of transportation even part of the time, then you're marginal. That's the way it works, and that's why we have various subcultural cliques that call themselves the "bike culture."

The worst part of all of it is that it's almost impossible to be just a regular person who rides a bike. If you drive for transportation and use your bicycle only for fitness and recreation then *maybe* you can, but certainly if you ride a bicycle to get around *at all* then you're one of the many cycling stereotypes that drivers hate. Meanwhile, cyclists also expect you to conform to one of the many cycling-based subcultures. It's like going to prison: The car is that big bald guy with all the Swastika tattoos who wants to kill you, and you feel like you have to join a gang in order to stay alive.

But none of this has to be, and we can and should abandon this whole bikes vs. cars thing along with the rest of our baggage. Since neither of these vehicles is going to go extinct, it's vital for us as cyclists to accept the fact that, ultimately, humankind is about as likely to forfeit its cars as it is its computers. It is important to acknowledge this motor vehicular indelibility for two reasons:

1. Denial is not healthy. I can hate the music of Billy Joel all I want (and I do), but at a certain point I need to come to terms with the fact that his music is deeply woven into our popular culture and that consequently I can't expect to avoid all contact with it. Like it or not, I'm going to hear it in the supermarket occasionally and I've got to make peace with that. I can't very well lose my temper, hit the dairy aisle, and smash up all the eggs. Similarly, if you ride your bike, you're going to come across cars, and as irritating as they can be, yelling at them and banging on them isn't going to help.

2. In refusing to acknowledge the driver's right to operate his or her vehicle, we are really being no better than the idiot who thinks cyclists are just overgrown children slowing traffic with our playthings and tells us to "Get on the sidewalk." It's easy to know deep in your heart that you're right and someone else is wrong. I know—*know*—that Billy Joel's "Italian Restaurant" is schmaltzy, treacly, and annoying, and that people who like it have poor taste. Similarly, plenty of cyclists know—*know*—that bicycles are clean and green and liberating, but cars are smoke-belching, resource-burning, Earth-killing machines. What's much harder, though—and much more important and necessary—is

realizing that, as Socrates said, "I know that I know nothing." Because as soon as you're right, someone else is wrong. And as soon as there's right and wrong, we're all in trouble. That's the moment at which Adam dons the fig leaf, Cain slays Abel, and human history becomes a series of wars between arbitrary forces of "good" and "evil."

Once we accept this, we, as the Chosen Commuters, can go about transcending all the transportation acrimony and creating a world in which neighbor shares the road with neighbor, and the delivery truck driver waves to the recumbent rider, and the recumbent rider fluffs his beard in gleeful greeting to the "Beautiful Godzilla" on the Dutch bike, and she in turn refrains from salmoning and nearly spearing some unfortunate pedestrian with the inevitable baguette in her basket, and so forth.

Of course, we must also do this in hope that noncycling drivers accept us as we accept them and that our cities and states work to accommodate us, yet we cannot count on this happening. The unfortunate truth is that the Infrastructure Gods giveth, and the Infrastructure Gods taketh away.

WHAT LIES BENEATH: VEHICULAR PREJUDICE

As cyclists we are oft ("oft" is pretentious for "often") the victims of vehicular prejudice. We can also be prejudiced ourselves, as is the cyclist who thinks that all drivers are evil by default.

But what of other vehicles? To reach true enlightenment, we must be willing to embrace all vehicles, and I'm here to tell you that it ain't going to be easy. (I'm certainly not there yet, since I wouldn't be caught dead doing most of these things.) Here are just a few oft-maligned vehicles we often find ourselves sharing the lanes with.

LONGBOARDS

Longboards are basically just long skateboards, and they're an increasingly common sight in big cities. They're similar to in-line skates in that they're basically just wheels you stand on, but they're also less threatening in that they move forward in a straight manner, like bicycles. Unfortunately, it's been my experience that they tend to move forward into you, since many longboarders are wanton salmoners. Also, longboarders tend to be almost unbearably "dudely" and laconic, which can be frustrating in a commuting context.

SEGWAYS

It's easy to feel contempt for these dork lecterns, these rolling nerd podiums, these Handtrucks of Hades, but why is that? Is it the fact that they're too fast and bulky for the sidewalk, yet too slow for the bike lane? Is it because of the smug manner in which the rider leans forward into the wind, like a dog sticking its head out of the window of a station wagon? Or is it just because we harbor a secret fear that the Segway is the vehicle of the future, and that in one fell and dorky swoop we seem to have undone millions of years of evolution by forfeiting our hard-won ability to walk?

Yes.

IN—LINE SKATERS

Pity the poor in-line skaters, like unto us in so many ways. They commute in traffic, they put on Lycra costumes in order to go fast, and they even play roller hockey, which is pretty much the same idea as bike polo. They also move completely under their own power, yet instead of having a machine between them and the road, they prefer to attach the wheels directly to their feet. Still, we ridicule them and reduce them to a single brand name—Rollerbladers—which would be like them calling us Cannondalers.

So what is it about in-line skaters that so threatens us? Well, really, it all comes down to the way they swing their arms back and forth to keep momentum going. As cyclists, even the worst of us moves forward in a straight-ish line, while trying to get around an in-line skater in a bike lane is like trying to slip past a running gorilla. Also, it's bad enough being drafted by another cyclist, but if you've ever been drafted by an in-line skater you know it's far more disconcerting, what with those swinging arms moving in and out of your peripheral vision like salamis in the wind.

RUNNERS

Sure, a runner is not a vehicle. Rather, a runner is a pedestrian who's exercising—and pedestrians warrant our utmost respect. However, since the runner is running for purposes of fitness or recreation (as opposed to extreme lateness or impending bear attack), this changes the dynamic considerably.

Runner/cyclist relationships are considerably strained. This is in part because we often share recreational lanes, and joggers tend to do frustrating things like stop suddenly in our paths and make abrupt about-faces while wearing headphones. Also, for some reason, our society has considerably more respect for runners than it has for cyclists. Marathon runners are fawned over by the local news media and celebrated for striving to exceed their "personal bests." Cyclists, on the other hand, are dismissed as Lycra-clad weekend warriors.

Runners can also be smug, but not for the reasons cyclists are smug. Runners are smug because they're fit individuals striving to improve their "personal bests," whereas cyclists are smug because they're "saving the Earth" by commuting in a "green" fashion. (Runners cannot make this claim as very few of them commute by running.) In either case, when smug fights smug, nobody wins.

Of course, somewhere in between we have triathletes, though they're more like double (or, technically, triple) agents and pretty much nobody trusts them.

ELECTRIC BICYCLES

There have been tremendous advances in electrically assisted bicycles recently. These have all sorts of benefits: everything from helping people with physical problems ride to facilitating hauling cargo by bike.

Unfortunately, there's also a tragic side effect, which is that they amplify poor cycling.

Think of the electric guitar—in the hands of a virtuoso it makes delightful sounds, but when played by a clod with ten thumbs it only increases the misery exponentially.

This is the case in New York City, where food-delivery people have embraced the electric bicycle and now power along the sidewalk at 20 mph instead of the mere 10 mph of which they were previously capable. And despite the fact that the bikes have batteries, I have yet to see a single one equipped with a light. This makes them veritable cruise missiles, except that their warheads consist mostly of bags of hot lo mein.

HEATHENDOM:
WHY PEOPLE DON'T RIDE

All of this talk of acceptance raises another question: If cyclists are the Chosen Commuters, should we proselytize? Does it make sense to try to convince people to live as we do and to embrace the bicycle? Is it even possible?

Even today, the idea of riding a bicycle simply as a mode of transportation is still a difficult one for most people to wrap their minds around, which is ironic because riding a bicycle simply as a mode of transportation is the kind of cycling that requires the least amount of thought. In one sense this is surprising, but in another sense it's perfectly logical since people tend to ignore the simplest solution. This is because if it's too cheap and there are no designer labels involved, they figure they are making a poor choice. It's the same reason people pay lots of money to buy Fiji water when all they have to do is turn on the tap and open their mouths.

So if people prefer to pay a premium for an essential component of life like water one liter at a time instead of partaking in a water system that would have left our thirsty, divining rod–wielding ancestors agog with astonishment, what hope does riding a bike have?

Like water, getting around is a necessity. Furthermore, bicycles are all around us, and like water they're relatively cheap (though fortunately unlike water they don't rain from the sky, since I wouldn't like to be hit in the head by a falling tandem). But instead of taking them for granted as we should and partaking of them without making a huge fuss about it, we prefer the designer-bottle approach. This tends to obfuscate the practical nature of cycling instead of revealing it.

This accounts for all those commuter fashions. It's also why, as a culture, we're far more comfortable with recreational and competitive cycling than we are with practical cycling. However, like Fiji water, when you think about it, this sort of cycling is kind of absurd, especially when it involves the following behaviors:

- Driving places to ride your bike;
- Obsessively tracking performance data such as mileage and wattage when you ride (otherwise known as the "if you can't download the ride, it didn't happen" approach);
- Considering any riding during which data is not monitored or during which you're not adhering to your training plan "junk miles."

None of this is to say I have anything whatsoever against recreational cycling; far from it. I am an eager fan of and participant in competitive bike racing, and a good deal of my riding is of the be-Lycraed variety. I have driven literally hundreds of miles in order to ride my bicycle in circles for forty-five minutes (this activity is known as "cyclocross") and, what's more, I don't feel in the least bit guilty about it. Not only did I have a good time, but I didn't harass any pedestrians or tell any of my fellow cyclists to "get on the sidewalk," and I believe that as long as you operate your vehicle compassionately and responsibly, it doesn't matter what kind of vehicle it is.

Still, cycling has sort of painted itself into a corner in a way (or, more accurately, stuffed itself into a skinsuit). When used recreationally, the bicycle is not really a vehicle; rather, it's a piece of sporting equipment, sharing more in common with a tennis racket or a pair of skis. Therefore, while most people in this country see using a bicycle for transportation as vaguely freakish, they do understand the bike as a piece of sporting equipment. What's more, it's a very popular piece of sporting equipment. Even though people have found bicycles annoying since the late nineteenth century, they remain way more popular than other pieces of sporting goods, including tennis rackets and skis. In fact, some estimates place cycling as the seventh most popular recreational activity in the United States. Apparently, the only recreational activities more popular are:

- Walking
- Swimming
- Camping
- Fishing
- Exercising with equipment (I assume this refers to weights, Bowflexes, Stairmasters, weird stomach-flattening apparatuses sold by Suzanne Somers, etc.)
- Bowling

So when you're riding to the store, you're kind of a freak engaging in "alternative transportation," but when you're climbing a hill in abject pain for no good reason whatsoever, you're engaging in the seventh most popular recreational pursuit in America. Seems like it should be the other way around.

So if cycling is indeed the seventh most popular form of pointless fitness activity in the country, then it's no accident, for the number seven is itself a highly significant number. It is the lowest number that cannot be represented as the sum of the square of three integers. (I have no idea what that means, but it's true.) According to Genesis (the Bible book, not the band), the Earth was created in seven days, and the Bible in general is positively rife with the number. There are seven deadly sins. It also happens to be the number of a subway train that will get you to Flushing. You may even recall George Carlin's famous list of the seven dirty words you can't say on television, which was:

- Shit
- Piss
- Fuck
- Cunt
- Cocksucker
- Motherfucker
- Tits

This is important, because the more common something is, the more we want to hide it—and the more complicated our relationship with it becomes. The fact that these words were forbidden says a lot about our society, inasmuch as all of them describe very common things—simple body parts, simple bodily functions, or simple sex acts—with the exception of "motherfucker," of course, which really is pretty nasty.

In any case, we're afraid of these words because, ever since we were evicted from the Garden of Eden, we've had a very uncomfortable relationship with our bodies and our desires. In fact, we're so uncomfortable that we can't even talk publicly about going to the bathroom. Our general uptightness is getting worse, too. Over two thousand years ago Sophocles wrote *Oedipus*, an entire play about a "motherfucker," and now we can't even say it. Clearly, for better or worse, we're getting more uptight as the years go on.

Similarly, you can also tell a lot about us from what constitutes our seven most popular recreational activities, and it's no accident that cycling is the seventh most popular among them. Once again, those activities are:

- Walking
- Swimming
- Camping
- Fishing
- Exercising with equipment
- Bowling
- Cycling

Like the seven dirty words, all of these are based on simple functions of life (with the exception of bowling, which is sort of the "motherfucker" of this list) from which we have distanced ourselves over the years. We've abstracted them and turned them into recreational activities that require special clothing and equipment. Walking, believe it or not, was something we once did to get from one place to the other. So, to a lesser extent, was swimming, though we also used it to dive for food and, most important, as a defense against drowning. Camping, of course, was simply living—back in the day, before houses and hotels, everybody camped by default. Fishing for its part was a means of sustenance, and sometimes used in conjunction with swimming. Exercising with equipment—or, as I prefer to call it, lifting heavy stuff—was, like camping, something we did as a matter of course (building pyramids, rescuing friends from avalanches, plowing, and so forth).

Bowling, on the other hand, was almost certainly a game from day one—I'm pretty sure it was never a form of hunting that eventually evolved into a recreational pursuit. That's why bowling is the "motherfucker" of the list. Like having sex with your mother, it's a societal construct, and a truly perverse form of pleasure that serves no practical purpose in nature.

And then, there's cycling. The bicycle as we know it was invented in the late nineteenth century, at a time in history during which working people were beginning to have something called "leisure time"—which they of course squandered by pitching tents even though they had perfectly good houses, swimming for fun instead of survival, and lifting heavy things voluntarily. For this reason, when the bicycle arrived, the leisure class went wild for it immediately and set to work exploiting its recreational capabilities, their pantaloons and handlebar moustaches fluttering majestically in the breeze. Cheap cars then arrived a few decades later, and so the pattern was set (at least in the United States) in the mind of the average person: bikes for fun, cars for transportation. At a key moment, Americans could have decided that the bicycle was a tool or that it was a toy. They went with toy.

So, then, back to the original question: Do we proselytize, and is it even possible?

The short answer is "No freaking way."

I say this as a lifelong lover of cycling who, in addition to recreating on a bike, uses a bicycle regularly for transportation and enjoys both practical and recreational cycling about as much as I enjoy almost anything else in the world. In fact, it's *because* I enjoy cycling so much that I know there's no freaking way most non-cycling people are suddenly going to start riding a bicycle, since it's my love of it that makes me put up with the indignity of cycling in a society that hates me for doing it and doesn't even want to give me my own tiny little lane.

Think about many of the people in your life, like your heavyset, cigar-chomping, middle-aged uncle with the Ford Explorer—you know, the one who's always making fun of your leaner, fitter uncle because he never got married and because he likes art. Now imagine this uncle riding a bicycle. You can't, unless you've seen YouTube videos of those Russian bicycling circus bears. It's just not going to happen, unless some ringmaster in a top hat and sequined waistcoat starts chasing him with a whip.

Even if everyone in your life *does* ride a bike, because you're one of those smug people who only hangs out with bikey people, or because you live in some weird place like Portland, just take a look around you the next time you're stopped at a red light. Go ahead, peek into everybody's car—just try to be subtle about it, so they don't call the police or try to taze you. Apart from maybe the student types in the hand-me-down Volvos and the wiry couples wearing LiveStrong bracelets and fleece vests driving Subarus with roof racks, almost everybody you see will be very difficult to imagine on a bike. They're wearing suits; they're ample of frame; they're sending e-mails and

putting on makeup and eating entire boxes of Chicken McNuggets. They're so ensconced in their cars that the notion of getting them out of their cars and onto bikes seems about as likely as extricating a conch from its roomy shell and coaxing it into a walnut.

This is because, over the generations, many of us have evolved to the point where we exist in symbiosis with our cars, and our ever-widening midsections fit tongue-and-groove with our bucket seats. Automobile companies spend millions of dollars on ad campaigns to try to convince people to change from one kind of car to another, and even *that* only works sometimes. So there's no way some well-meaning public service announcements and some newspaper editorials about saving gas money are going to get anybody to change from a car to a *bike*.

Then again, not everything is as it seems, and as a wise person with a beard once said, "Judge not, lest you be judged"—which is yet another reason why *American Idol* is one of our greatest cultural evils.

As mollusk-like as our relationship with our cars has become, and as annoying as we find bicycles and cyclists to be, cycling is nevertheless ingrained in us, and as much a part of us as any of the seven dirty words (excluding, perhaps, the incestual one). It's our relationship with bikes that's strained, and as soon as people feel comfortable, those bicycles come out of the closet like a million Ricky Martins.

Take the building in which I live, for example. It's a surly bunch with whom I cohabit, and their chief pastime appears to be smoking cigarettes under the awning and not holding the door for you. It's hard to imagine *any* of them riding a bicycle, and I always felt rather out of place as I struggled to enter the building with my bicycle as they stood there smoking and silently hating me.

However, to my surprise, at a building-wide meeting one day it emerged that not only did many of my neighbors have bicycles, but they wanted a place to store them, and so we adapted a bit of outside space. Lo and behold, that section of real estate filled up with bicycles more quickly than Ricky Martin's inbox filled up with date requests after he came out—and they *use* the bikes, too. In fact, it turns out my superintendent actually runs errands on his bicycle when he's not glowering at me and trying to run me over in the hallway with the vacuum cleaner. I had simply judged him too quickly, figuring that somebody that profoundly ornery couldn't possibly ride a bicycle.

Moreover, no one had to coax these people into riding. We didn't have to offer "carbon offsets" or "green credits" or provide everybody with a handmade lugged steel commuter bike and matching designer waxed-cotton cycling cap, either. We just had to knock down a relatively minor barrier and they took care of the rest themselves.

You can't—or at least shouldn't—try to make somebody do something they don't want to do. People don't like it. At the same time, though, you can make it easier for people to do something they want to do but feel like nobody wants them to do. Cycling is one of those things. On a personal level, we can do our part as cyclists by not being insular or overly aggressive and by not buzzing pedestrians or hitting cars. On a municipal level, more bike lanes would be nice, but at the same time we've got to be prepared to ride anyway, since their presence may very well be fleeting—like a rainbow, or an aura of smugness. To a certain extent, we've got to think of cycling like a big prison escape—we're digging our way out with our spoons, so every time we leave our cell we've got to take a pocketful of dirt with us. This pocketful of dirt is the goodwill you express on each ride, and if we all do our tiny part, we may get to the other side of the wall where commuting paradise lies.

What we can't do, however, is try to overpower the guards in some Attica of Annoyance, which is what Critical Mass is. Whether it's worshipping a specific god or pushing an acquired taste on a stranger ("You simply *must* try this head cheese!"), we are irresistibly compelled to try to shove the things we like down others' throats. Jesus or Jell-O, we foist it on our neighbors, and the results are almost always (predictably) disastrous. It's yet another tragedy of the human condition.

And when it comes to this sort of behavior, cyclists are as bad as it gets. I was reading an online review about a certain cargo bike, partially because I find cargo bikes interesting, but mostly because I find the things the kinds of people who ride cargo bikes say to be funny. In one of the comments, somebody criticized a certain cargo bike because it "isn't really that appealing for someone who normally drives an SUV." *No* bicycle is appealing for someone who normally drives an SUV, I don't care how SUV-like it is! You don't coax someone out of a Navigator and onto a *Bakfeits*. You'd be better off trying to sell people tempeh at a rib joint.

In this sense, insisting that people should trade their SUVs for cargo bikes is about as reasonable and considerate as drivers insisting that cyclists shouldn't have their own lanes. Not everybody needs to leave the prison. Some people have been institutionalized, and that's totally fine. Instead, the focus should be on helping them understand why your cycling is better for *them*—and it is. If they can understand that having to watch out for cyclists costs them absolutely no time, and in fact that a person who's riding instead of driving is one less car to cause traffic or hog that fuel pump, then maybe they'll drop the animosity and get behind us. (In the good way, not in the "I didn't see you, sorry I ran you over" way.)

In the early days of Christianity, before the whole thing went mainstream, there were a bunch of indie Christians called Gnostics. The Gnostics were, in their day, total hipsters, and were almost certainly completely insufferable, full of themselves, and annoying to be around. Doubtless, they were intolerably smug, and I'm sure Gnosticism is poised for a resurgence in Portland if it hasn't happened already. Anyway, the Gnostics believed that there were three types of people: hylics, psychics, and pneumatics.

1. **HYLICS:** These were the lowest order of people, those who would never "get it." In the Gnostic times, it meant they'd never reach enlightenment. In Portland Gnosticism 2.0

times, it means they're totally uncool, shop at Walmart, wear football jerseys, and watch *American Idol* unironically.

2. **PSYCHICS:** These were the people who were partly spiritual but had not managed to separate themselves fully from the material plane. In Gnostic times, that probably meant holding a "straight" job like repairing sandals, but showing up at the occasional Gnostic freakout on weekends. Now it means working in consulting, but having an easily concealed tattoo, wearing trendy sneakers on casual Fridays, and possibly visiting SXSW or Burning Man.

3. **PNEUMATICS:** These were the highest order of humans. A Gnostic Pneumatic could probably perform miracles, levitate, or turn water into hummus. Today, the Pneumatic Portlander would probably be so transcendently ironic that he or she could untangle someone's dreadlocks with the force of his or her will.

Apart from understanding hipsters, I also find Gnosticism to be a very useful template when it comes to understanding cycling. The Hylics are the people we just looked at—the root-bound (or, more accurately, "ass-bound") SUV drivers who will never know cycling.

Shower them with love, don't let them kill you, and move on.

The Psychics are the more complicated bunch. These are the people who like to say they would ride their bikes to work and for transportation generally, and maybe even ride recreationally already, but have a whole bunch of excuses as to why they don't. As I said, we should remove as many obstacles as possible, but we can't move mountains either. Some of these Psychics, like my neighbors, will actually ride if things are a little easier for them. Others, however, feel that an entire series of prerequisites must be fulfilled before they do. They're the "cock teases" of cycling advocacy, to use a crude colloquialism, and they're really only saying they'd ride bikes because you're *supposed* to—just like Tom Segura acknowledges it's "healthy and green" because he's *supposed* to. Here are some of the more common excuses of the Cycling Psychic.

"I would ride to work if I had a safe place to park my bike."

This is the excuse that bothers me the most, because what it really means is, "I want to ride a fancy bike to work and I can't because someone might take it, so instead I'll ride nothing at all." First of all, cars get stolen all the time too, and people regularly park cars that cost over $50,000 on the street. Second of all, if people are worried about their bikes getting stolen, *why not just ride crappy bikes?* My neighbors sure do—it's a real scrap heap out there, and every time I get my own bike I'm afraid I'll get tetanus.

I hate theft as much as anybody, and I'd love it if there were more safe bike parking, but that seems like something we should focus on addressing after more important issues, like *making it so we can ride without getting killed.* Once that's done, maybe we can fuss over the details. In the meantime, we should divorce ourselves from our attachment to the object, and saying you're not going to ride to work until there's no risk of your bike getting stolen is like saying you're not going to have sex until the world is completely rid of STDs. Sure, it's safer, but at a certain point you've got to think of your quality of life. Precaution is more fun than abstinence, after all.

"I would ride if I could do so without getting killed."

Okay, this one's a little more understandable. Depending on where you live, opting to commute by bike may be a daunting proposition. Someone who loves to ride will launch a bicycle into any stream of traffic like a pro kayaker hitting class 5 rapids, but for the so-called "normal person" this may not seem like a reasonable thing to do.

At the same time, though, if nobody rides in the first place, then where's the momentum to add traffic amenities for bikes? And even if they do add them, who says that the Psychics aren't going to move on to some other precondition, like safe parking for their brand-new randonneur bikes, or machines that control the weather—which, of course brings us to the next common excuse:

"I would ride if it wasn't for foul/hot/cold weather."

This one's easy: don't ride in foul/hot/cold weather if you don't want to. Depending on where you live, this still leaves anywhere from 100 to 365 bikeable days a year. Plus, you're riding a crappy bike anyway, so if it starts raining in the middle of the day you can just leave it locked up where it is, since who's going to want to steal such a crappy bike? The notion that you have to use the same vehicle day in and day out is brainwashing fallout from the bikes vs. cars wars. Nobody has to ride a bike every day.

"I have to look nice for work."

This excuse should be the most trivial one, but in a way it's actually the most ironclad, and that's why it makes me more angry than all the others. We now live in the twenty-first century. (Well, excluding people like the Amish, the Taliban, and Larry King.) For the most part, we've managed to shed all sorts of primitive notions: that illness is cured by bloodletting, that the Sun revolves around the Earth, that Charlie Sheen can stay sober. However, we just can't seem to shed this whole "costume" thing.

Arguably, costumes hit their peak back in the 1700s, when people used to wear crazy curly powdered wigs and shirts with wildly ruffled cuffs, but even as recently as the twentieth century people still couldn't even go to the beach without wearing garments that were at least as complicated as the typical modern-day wedding dress.

Since then, we've come a long way, and yesterday's underwear is today's tuxedo. Still, even though we can wear jeans and T-shirts most of the time like a bunch of filthy nineteenth-century laborers, many of us are still expected to wear all kinds of superfluous items of clothing to our jobs, and this is, quite frankly, ridiculous.

Does a lawyer really do a better job because he's wearing a suit?

Barring emergency tourniquet application, what purpose does a necktie serve?

Is there even a point to "business casual"? Isn't that like being "a little bit vegetarian"?

Frankly, as far as the workplace goes, there hasn't been a loosening of the dress code worth mentioning since Susan B. Anthony got women wearing pants, and that's sad. Consequently, our society is literally prisoner to its own wardrobe. What could be more pleasant than riding a bicycle to work on a warm summer day, and what could be more fundamental than the freedom to make that decision? Unfortunately, many of us can't because we're required to dress like it's 40 degrees when it's 80 degrees, and to stay that way all day, and not to let our bodies belie the absurdity of this pretense by sweating or emitting any natural odors.

Instead, our entire transportation infrastructure is based on transporting us in a climate-controlled environment that allows us to look like walking (or, more accurately, sitting) advertisements for the Burlington Coat Factory.

This is not our fault—we all need to work, jobs can be hard to come by, and you'd be foolish to flirt with your livelihood by being the one employee in a sweat-stained T-shirt. At the same time, it isn't until we move forward and embrace our fundamental slovenliness and organic humanity that we will be free to transport ourselves as effectively and efficiently as possible, regardless of vehicle choice. Really, when you think about it, the only people who need to wear special things to work are:

- The Police—It's only fair that we should see them coming.
- People who handle dangerous items on a regular basis— This should go without saying; you can't handle plutonium in a wifebeater.
- Prisoners—Otherwise, things get too confusing.
- Clergy, nuns, monks, and other religious devotees— Because it's just not religion without all the crazy vestments.
- Boy bands—Because it's classy when they match.

Otherwise, the rest of us should be more or less free to wear what we want (or not wear what we want). After all, most of the financial sector dresses pretty formally, as do most people in real estate, and look how well all of that turned out.

Yes, some companies do go so far as to offer their workers showers and lockers to encourage (or at least not actively discourage) them to commute by bicycle, but as far as I'm concerned, this is just a patch that fails to address the fundamental problem. Do you shower at the bar when you ride your bike to have a drink with friends? Probably not. Then why should you have to do it when you get to work?

BOOK
IV

TRANSCENDENCE

THE ALCHEMY OF
THE MUNDANE

There's lots of talk these days about "sustainability." The Environmental Protection Agency defines sustainability as enacting "policies and strategies that meet society's present needs without compromising the ability of future generations to meet their own needs." For example, if you pull all the fish out of the ocean, then they can't have fishy sex and make more little fishies for our children to eat. Therefore, there are laws about how many we can take, because the world is not an all-you-can-eat buffet. It's only common sense.

People are especially interested in sustainability when they are shopping, because while they may or may not have a real understanding of where the stuff they buy comes from and how it is made, they do want to be sure that it is made in the right way—and by "right" they mean "sustainably." This means we don't have to feel guilty about buying it.

In particular, we're often most concerned about sustainability when the thing we're paying for is unnecessary or a luxury, such as a meal in a restaurant. This is where sustainability sells best. None of us really *needs* to eat out, so when we do we like to convince ourselves that we're performing a public service. Transforming self-indulgence into a *mitzvah* is perhaps the greatest human accomplishment of the twenty-first century.

Sustainability comes up especially often if you're interested in bicycles. Many cyclists love to congratulate themselves for engaging in a theoretically sustainable mode of transit, and for wearing boutique clothing made out of sustainable fabrics, and for eating sustainable comestibles and other forms of sustainable sustenance in sustainable vegan cafés.

Oddly, though, we don't seem to be as interested in sustainability when it comes to our own mental and emotional well-being. We hear plenty about the importance of composting, turning wind into energy, and recycling our waste, and we're supposed to feel guilty about squandering those resources. However, nobody ever talks about the fact that we're squandering our most precious emotional resource, which is our happiness.

In terms of transport, sustainability is relative. Happiness, on the other hand, is absolute. Everything flows forth from our happiness, including the desires to be munificent, to improve our surroundings, and to please others. When you're miserable, the last thing you're thinking about is giving back to the world. Mostly, you just want to kick it in the nuts.

Unfortunately, much of the time we burn something on the way to work that's arguably even more precious than oil or hummus: little chunks of our goodwill. This happens every time we get exasperated, get cut off, cut somebody off, or embroil ourselves in an altercation with our fellow commuters. If your car runs out of gas, it sputters and dies. If your body runs out of hummus, you get dizzy and pass out. And if your brain runs out of goodwill, you become one of those cranky, miserable people who take out their crankiness and misery on everybody around them.

In fact, your commute probably consists mostly of cranky and miserable people, who in turn make you cranky and miserable, and together we form a cranky miserable society that argues about whose streets these are and who's the bigger douchebag. It's basically an arms race of irritability, and it started at the very tip of the Dachshund of Time's tail. Just as drivers buy more and more horsepower so they can overpower their fellow commuters, so do we all have to yell that much louder in order to drown out our cranky and miserable neighbors. The entire enterprise is eminently unsustainable from a metaphysical standpoint. No wonder people are getting hurt.

Happiness can seem as unsustainable as oil. Even though we all long for it, and even though it's our most basic shared need besides feeding ourselves, we seem to have a lot of trouble finding it. That's why there are lots of people and organizations that will claim they can make you happy. Various religions will tell you that if you follow their rules about dieting and refraining from touching yourself, you will find happiness. Minimalists will tell you that if you divest yourself of your excess possessions, you will find happiness. And companies will tell you that if you acquire their sustainable, eco-friendly products, you will find happiness.

The problem, however, is that most of these methods are not sustainable either. They're like drilling for oil—you might hit a gusher, but eventually it's going to run out and leave behind only a scar.

Knowing that you're going to heaven because you never masturbate on Sundays, or whatever, can make you happy, but it also comes at the expense of thinking everybody else is wrong.

Minimalism might seem liberating at first, but after a while obsessing about the stuff you don't own becomes as distracting as obsessing over the stuff you do. It's like going "commando," in that the freedom feels good when you start out, but after a while the chafing sets in.

As for finding happiness in shopping, you might get a short-lived thrill over that new purchase, but in the long run it can ruin you, since even the best heath insurance doesn't cover retail therapy—and money is like a forest, in that it takes very little time to burn it but quite a while for it to grow back.

Wouldn't it be great, then, if we could find an eternally gushing well of sweet, soothing, my-spleen-is-practically-vibrating-with-joy happiness? What if we could just turn all this anger, hate, rage, crankiness, and irritability into joy? Wouldn't it be like having a perpetual motion machine? Wouldn't the overflow of goodwill ultimately buoy all of humanity?

Well, maybe or maybe not, but I maintain that we can at least find genuine, guilt-free, renewable happiness that will make life better for ourselves and for everybody around us, provided we simply adopt a philosophy of "mental greenness." I don't mean that we should all smoke tons of marijuana, although given some of the pissed-off people we share the streets with, filling their cars with heady, TCH-laden smoke would probably help. (It would be like that scene in *History of the World: Part I* when Josephus outwits the Romans with Mighty Joint.) No, what I mean is that we need to learn how to compost our misery.

We've all got plenty of misery—often more than we think we can dispose of safely. In particular, we're all burdened with pain-in-the-ass chores, pain-in-the-ass employers, and pain-in-the-ass things we don't want to do. We need to go back and forth to work to earn a paycheck, we need to make appointments with dentists, physicians, shrinks, and karate instructors, and we need to spend our paychecks on suitably sustainable and eco-friendly products so that when we open our cupboards we can feel good about ourselves.

Moreover, for most of us the process of getting crap like this done consumes most of our day, and the stress, irritation, and weariness that comes with it are a large part of why we're so unhappy. However, if you can turn this business of getting crap done into fun, you can turn those pain-in-the-ass chores and that pain-in-the-ass job and all the concomitant stress and irritation into joy—and having an abundance of joy in your life ultimately results in happiness.

Centuries ago, people tried to turn lead into gold with no success. However, it turns out you can turn the drudgery of getting crap done into happiness.

It's the Alchemy of the Mundane.

If you enjoy riding a bicycle, you're probably already a lot more of a mundanity alchemist than the typical horn-honking, accelerator-stomping SUV pilot. However, the beauty of the Alchemy of the Mundane is that you can constantly refine it. I've always loved to ride my bike, and it's always been a huge source of joy for me, but I wasn't always so adept at injecting that joy into all the various areas of my life. For a long time, I didn't think to enjoy a practical ride since it merely reminded me that I wasn't on a recreational ride. I was on a crappy, beat-up bike instead of my immaculate racing bike; I was on city streets instead of rolling country hills; I was wearing everyday clothes instead of special stretch moisture-wicking vestments.

In short, I was so distracted by the way real riding differed from my platonic idea of riding that I forgot that I was still *riding*, and that distraction was the difference between misery and happiness.

Over the years, though, this began to change. I realized that wishing you were riding while you're actually riding is like missing somebody you live with and looking at her picture while she's sitting right next to you on the couch. This makes both you and your partner very unhappy. Similarly, I realized that the idealistic version of riding I constantly longed for was actually making me unhappy, because the expensive bike and specialized wardrobe it required were completely incompatible with everyday life and impossible to integrate into the misery of Getting Crap Done. It was like that *Seinfeld* episode where Kenny Bania insists that Jerry owes him a meal but won't count the enjoyable lunch they're having in a diner:

"The soup counts," explains Jerry. "That's the meal."

It was the same thing with riding—the bike commute counts, that's the ride. It's up to you to enjoy it. It certainly doesn't preclude those fancy, platonic, ideal, racing bike recreational rides, either. I still enjoy those too—actually, I probably enjoy them more, because they're effectively a bonus.

But when it comes to mastering the Alchemy of the Mundane, learning to derive joy from even the most menial forms of cycling and then to infuse that joy into as much of your life as possible is the easy part, and most cyclists have figured it out already—apart from roadies, that is, who are in thrall to their false belief in junk miles. The harder part is the training.

Yes, unfortunately, the Alchemy of the Mundane requires training, though unlike competitive cycling, this isn't physical training. Rather, it's training yourself to happily enter that great communal living room that is the Great Wide World, to run the gauntlet through it as you're constantly beaten by the miserable, unhappy people who are your fellow human beings, and to emerge happily from it when you get to the other end.

This is harder than the steepest hill repeats, or the most intense intervals, or the most groin-numbingly tedious indoor training session you've ever experienced. It's relatively easy to keep your head down and pedal until it hurts, but it's not that easy to maintain your contentment when someone throws their car door open in front of you or tells you that you belong on the sidewalk.

When physical training gets hard, all you have to do is quit, and there are really no consequences. However, when maintaining the Alchemy of the Mundane becomes difficult and you quit, you often do so by hurling an obscenity at somebody, and as tantalizing as this impulse is, I don't think there's anybody who has reacted well to being told to go fuck himself. In the best case scenario, you might find someone who takes it literally and actually tries to go fuck himself, but even that will almost certainly end regrettably.

So what does this training actually involve? Well, commuting is a lot more like trying to walk along the floor of a sludgy pond while wearing lead boots than we realize, and the most aerodynamic bicycle is not going to change that, since most of the resistance we're encountering is the by-product of the actions of what lay people call "assholes." I'm far from mastering the Alchemy of the Mundane myself— if I had mastered it, I wouldn't need to commute anywhere and could simply sit at home levitating and untangling people's dread-locks. Actually, when I set out on a ride I feel like Samuel Jackson's character in *Pulp Fiction*—a dangerously irritable person who's trying reeeal hard to be the shepherd. However, I find the following tricks to be helpful, and with practice my commutes have become far more pleasurable.

ZERO OUT YOUR MENTAL COMPUTER

If there's one thing we've learned from the history of commuting, it's how important it is to leave your baggage behind when embarking upon a journey. Obviously this doesn't apply to literal baggage, and if you want to take to the streets in a *Bakfeits* laden with 150 pounds of coleslaw as well as the entire contents of your underwear drawer, that's perfectly fine with me. Rather, I mean that you have to leave behind your *mental* baggage. You might be really angry at your boss, but if you carry that anger with you, it means you're going to get that much closer to that stupid jaywalker who should have the good sense to stay on the sidewalk—you know, that slab of concrete where all the drivers say you belong. Also, you need to divest yourself of anxiety before setting out, especially if one of the things you're anxious about is getting where you're going quickly. Entering the Great Wide World in a hurry is like trying to fish quickly; not only will you enjoy the process more if you take your time, but savoring the aspect you can control greatly improves the odds that the aspect you can't control will turn out a lot better.

At the same time, you can't be naïve, either. This is the Great Wide World we're talking about, and something may very well go wrong. If it were totally predictably benign, then we could just leave the house naked with no money. Therefore, you have to temper your expectations and know that you're liable to encounter something irritating. This is a tricky balance, because if you don't expect this, you'll be taken off guard when it happens, yet if you set out on your commute looking for trouble, you're guaranteed to find it. Personally, I find it helpful to approach my commute like I do a frozen pizza or an episode of *Saturday Night Live*—I don't expect much, so I'm usually pleasantly surprised when it's not totally awful.

TELEPATHIC HANDLING

thIS BIKE GOES WHERE YOU POINT It.

LATERALLY STIFF yet verticaI compLiant

READ BICYCLE REVIEWS BUT SUBTRACT THE BIKE

If you've read more than one bicycle review, you're familiar with most of the clichés:

- "This bike goes where you point it,"
- "Telepathic handling," and of course,
- "Laterally stiff yet vertically compliant."

Obviously, all of these are ridiculous. What bike that is properly assembled *doesn't* go where you point it? Sure, when you get a shopping cart with a wonky wheel, that might not go where you point it, but odds are you're not riding a bicycle in a state of similar disrepair.

As for telepathic handling, of *course* the bike has telepathic handling. It's not like an old-timey ship where the captain had to yell down to the guys shoveling coal into the furnaces and tell them "Full speed ahead!" On a bike—any bike, not just a race bike—you pretty much think it and it happens. You don't have to actually talk to your legs.

And "laterally stiff yet vertically compliant" is just the sort of self-contradicting phrase that sounds deep and Zen and makes people nod knowingly and say, "Yesss, I must have that." It's like *A Shot in the Dark*, when Inspector Clouseau says, "I believe everything and I believe nothing. I suspect everyone and I suspect no one." It's a fine line between "Zen" and "Meh," and bike reviews tend toward the latter.

Bike reviews are useful, though, because they inadvertently tell you *how* to ride, in that all they're doing is ascribing a rider's natural actions to the bicycle so that you want to buy it. A bike *will* go where you point it, so aim carefully. A bike *will* handle telepathically, so don't think about how you want to buzz that pedestrian to make a point about jaywalking. And a rider *should* be "laterally stiff and vertically compliant," in that you should ride confidently and own your portion of the road, but not to the degree that you're unable to yield when it's warranted.

Essentially, we've reached a point where we've personified the bike to the extent that we defer to it, and we forget our own jobs. Want to be fast? Buy a fast bike. Want to be an elegant, cycle-chic commuter? Buy an elegant, cycle-chic bike. But even the most elegant-looking bike will perform like a wonky-wheeled shopping cart if it's piloted by a clod. We need to reclaim the ideals that bike companies and reviewers ascribe to bikes and apply them to ourselves. We should go where we point ourselves, we should communicate telepathically with ourselves, and we should be laterally stiff and vertically compliant—but to credit those things to a bike is like saying your shirt has personality or your television is creative.

Oh, and watch out for thieves too—otherwise it will "disappear beneath you," which is another bike review cliché.

SET GOALS

Generally, I don't believe in having goals. Rules were made to be broken, goals were meant to be missed, and if I wanted to set myself up for disappointment, I'd just invite a rabid gorilla over for a quiet, sociable evening. Plus, working toward a single goal can actually be distracting, since if you focus on one goal too intently, you might wind up inadvertently foregoing another. You've got to have direction, but you've also got to be open-minded. What if Nathaniel Hawthorne had abandoned *The Scarlet Letter* because it interfered with his duties at the Boston Custom House?

However, one area in which goals can be helpful is in bicycle commuting. In particular, I find it helpful to set out on my journey with two goals in mind:

1. Not to get killed.
2. To make it all the way to my destination without getting angry.

The first goal, obviously, is common sense—unless you're a suicide bomber, wanting to get to where you're going without getting killed is pretty much a given.

The second goal, however, is a lot more difficult, and far more often than not I fail at it spectacularly—though with practice I get a little bit better at it all the time. With my mental computer zeroed out (easy to do, since I'm what you might euphemistically call "simple-minded"), I imagine the happiness I'm feeling at that moment as a great big bowl of Froot Loops, brimming with sugary milk, and it's my job to portage this bowl across town without spilling any of that sickly-sweet Kellogg's deliciousness. Of course, as I said, I often fail at this and have at times dumped the Froot Loops all over someone else's head in a fit of rage, but I'm trying *reeeal hard* to be the shepherd.

I also find it helpful when pursuing Goal #2 to remember my experiences on September 11 and to keep in mind that, underneath it all, we're all in pursuit of Goal #1, and this is comforting—though unfortunately some people are more haphazard with their Froot Loops than others.

EMBRACE NEGATIVITY

Even though I go through my commute trying to balance a big bowl of Froot Loops, that does not mean I'm some sappy, saccharine, ingenuous dupe. On the contrary, I am a dupe that is as full of negativity and bubbling tar–like primordial blackness as anybody else. To deny this would be to deny my fundamental humanity, and to say that it comes from somewhere else or to deny responsibility is even more ludicrous than those bike reviews that personify bicycles by imbuing them with mystical powers.

There's no Satan, regardless of how menacingly omnipresent Oprah may seem.

More important, just like cars, this collective sludge of negativity is not going away anytime soon. So rather than trying to sublimate it, or deny it, or ignore it, we should try to understand it and embrace it—not through confrontation, attacks, obscenities, or Froot Loop–hurling, but through analysis and humor. That was the whole point of George Carlin's "Seven Dirty Words."

I think it's perfectly fine to be disgusted by something, provided you take the time to understand why it disgusts you. I also believe that as cyclists we should rise above negativity as much as we can, but what we can't rise above we should wallow in, for that is the only way to ford the Rubicon of unhappiness.

The best path to self-actualization is not to Become Your Dream; rather, it's to Come to Terms with Your Nightmare. If you think you hate something, it's probably because it reminds you of something inside yourself. Take a long look, and figure out what that is.

PRACTICE GOOD COMMUTING DEEDS

The world has an irritating way of failing to conform to our expectations, and this is especially true of commuting. When millions of people all want to go in different directions at the same time, it's inevitable that at least two of those people are going to crash into each other. Ideally, you don't want to be one of those people, but regardless of how adeptly you weave your way through this ganglion of humanity, ultimately there's no accounting for the stupidity or inattention of your fellow human beings. You can steer yourself, but you can't steer them.

One thing you do have absolute control over, though, is how you treat other people. As the Bible says, "Do unto others as you would have them do unto you." This is also known as the Golden Rule. However, while it may be golden, like any rule it's only as good as the people who follow it, and there's always a loophole.

In the case of this particular rule, the problem is that we're essentially a self-obsessed and self-gratifying culture, so too often following the Golden Rule just means we end up masturbating each other the same way we masturbate ourselves. Take Critical Mass for example. It's easy as a cyclist to treat another cyclist well, since for the most part we like them already because they're on a bike, and a bunch of people riding together to help the cause of cycling may seem selfless, but it's essentially just a big circle jerk—and there's your masturbatory loophole. Of course we *should* like each other, but we shouldn't *delude* each other.

A far more difficult yet far more edifying good deed is treating someone else well for no good reason at all. This can be incredibly satisfying, but unfortunately it also goes against every instinct we have as the miserable human beings that we are. This is why letting a stranger cut in front of you in traffic can make you feel like a complete sucker—the equivalent of e-mailing your checking account number and PIN to a Nigerian prince. This is also why, in the Great

Wide World, the spectrum of interaction generally ranges between indifference and "go fuck yourself." Therefore, in order to do good deeds for fellow commuters, we need to sort of trick ourselves into it.

PETE TOWNSHEND

Personally, I take perverse delight in confounding people's expectations, and this is especially easy to do as a cyclist because everyone expects you to break traffic laws like Pete Townshend used to break guitars. (I don't know if Pete Townshend still breaks guitars—he's pretty old now, so I imagine the only thing he's breaking these days is his hip.)

Over the years, I've become much better about stopping at red lights on my bicycle, and at a certain point I noticed that when I did it pedestrians seemed far more confused than when I used to run them. As I rolled up to the light and came to a gentle stop, the pedestrians would eye me quizzically, sometimes halting or even jumping, as though I might suddenly change my mind and decide to lunge at them. It was like they were gazelles and I was a suspiciously disinterested lion who was about to realize, "Hey, what am I doing? I'm a lion! I'd better tear this gazelle's throat out." When I didn't, they'd then flash me a disappointed look and continue, like I was some kind of idiot—in fact, they seemed almost annoyed that I hadn't tried to run them down.

And that was the best part—the fact that I had annoyed them. Let's be honest, it can be fun to be annoying, so what could be better than annoying people while following the law? It's a win-win! Not all pedestrians were skittish though—the older ones were more accusing. They'd sort of squint menacingly at me as I stopped as if daring me to attack. Then, when I didn't attack, they'd look at me contentedly—not the contentment that comes with gratitude, but rather the contentment that comes with victory. "That's right, stay where you are, you scoundrel!" the looks seemed to say. And who could blame them? After years of molestation at the hands of inconsiderate cyclists, they were now savoring the cyclist's comeuppance.

When I started noticing this, I realized something: Sure, it was fun to annoy people who were annoyed by cyclists not being annoying, but it was even more fun to watch the way people go so quickly from fear to dominance and how the oppressed so quickly becomes the oppressor.

But what *really* made me start to enjoy stopping at lights was when, after a while, I started encountering sincere, guileless gratitude. That sort of thing will melt your heart—even if it's a hardened hunk of expired processed cheese like mine is. I'll never forget stopping at a red light during the evening rush hour in Manhattan as an elderly man slowly crossed the street. As I did so he turned to me in amazement that quickly turned to sweetness:

"Thank you for stopping. What a beautiful young man."

I wasn't even a young man at the time, and I certainly wasn't beautiful then or arguably ever, but even so, the words actually touched me. I thought about what a pain in the ass it probably was for him to shuffle around town as pedestrians crowded him and cars cut him off and bicycles buzzed him, and with one considerate act I may very well have changed the entire tenor of his day.

Either that or he was a creepy old pervert, but I prefer the other scenario.

Anyway, since that day I've actually encountered plenty of people, some creepier than others, who have thanked me or congratulated me for the simple act of stopping at a light. This is New York City, mind you, where we don't give each other credit for anything. Crossing guards, guys driving Con Ed trucks, weird people walking tiny dogs. It's sort of sad that something so simple even warrants thanks—it's like thanking someone for not pissing on your leg—but it feels good nonetheless.

In fact, it feels so good that I've extended my courtesy to accommodating people beyond intersections. Sure, I won't deny I used to take pleasure in shooting through a crowd of jaywalkers in such a perfectly timed way as to startle them without hitting anybody. At the same time though, there's more pleasure in spotting someone who's clearly having a pretty difficult time of things and letting her through. Not only does it make you happy, but there's one less person leaving a comment on some news article or blog post about how inconsiderate cyclists are, or voting for some city councilman who's pushing some ridiculous proposal to make people register their bikes and get cycling licenses.

Again—and I cannot stress this enough—this is not to say that I'm some benign cycling being. I'm sure even on my best day I manage to irritate three people to every one I edify. Still, I keep practicing, and it's the practice that's important. Practice doesn't make perfect, but it does engender more practice, and that's good enough.

IT'S THE THOUGHT THAT COUNTS

I believe doing each one of these things, or trying to, or even *thinking* about it before setting out on your commute is worth a thousand Critical Mass participations or a million self-righteous forum posts. Everyone practicing this sort of thing is what greens the Great Wide World.

This is much more important than this whole supposedly green business of supporting or vilifying people based on the relative cleanliness of their vehicle choice. Actually, I think one of the biggest mistakes cycling advocates have made is tethering it to the green movement and using that as its basis. Not only does people's interest in green wax and wane, but what happens when cars *do* become really green? "Finally, clean cars—now we can at last get rid of those stupid bike lanes."

Who would you rather share the road with? A compassionate and considerate person in a Hummer, or an arrogant, self-absorbed cyclist?

BE AWARE OF SOCIAL ONANISM

One day, I was riding my bicycle through Brooklyn's Prospect Park, as I often do. Like any large public space in which people recreate, Prospect Park is a veritable Petri dish of human interaction, full of walkers and runners and cyclists and cross-country rollerskiers and horseback riders and dog walkers and even some weird guy who walks around and around the park kicking a gigantic rubber ball. This is to say nothing of what goes on in the woods or behind clumps of shrubbery. If people do it for fun, they do it in Prospect Park.

As I rode around the park loop in a leisurely fashion, I was overtaken by the local training crew. Resplendent in their Lycra finery, they went by at quite a clip, their expensive carbon-fiber race bikes making an impressive wooshing sound as they passed. A go-fast cyclist myself, I've certainly been part of such groups, and I noted how different they seem when you're not actually in them. When you're thrumming along, your legs and bicycle in perfect concert, some type-A dentist or lawyer blocking the wind in front of you, it all seems incredibly orderly. You communicate with subtle hand signals, you point out obstacles to each other, and you silently scoff at the awkward people in sweatpants veering unpredictably all over the park road.

But when you're not part of the group and they zip by you, coming within inches of some young child taking his first tentative spin on a bicycle, they mostly just look like a bunch of hormone-addled idiots.

Shortly after they passed me and continued weaving through the children and the speedwalkers and the elderly and the surly teens on skateboards, they encountered a roller skater in the middle of the road. Not a Rollerblader or user of any other brand of in-line skates, but a guy on actual 1970s-style four-wheeled roller skates. Not only that, but he was actually disco-skating, roller-sashaying forward for a few yards and then suddenly spinning around with a dramatic wave of his arms so that he was skating backward, wiggling his hips like he had something stuck to the seat of his pants and he was trying to dislodge it. He was also wearing headphones, which were presumably blaring Gloria Gaynor, or KC and the Sunshine Band, or some other similarly appropriate roller-disco soundtrack.

You'd be surprised at how much disco skating there is in twenty-first century New York.

So here come the bike racers, ten or fifteen men on $5,000 hunks of Taiwanese carbon, and while they're quite used to avoiding the usual park obstacles, they simply can't account for the disco rhythms that are driving Rollerguy. One second he's going frontward, the next he's going backward, then suddenly he's darting side to side like a goalie anticipating a puck, and then without warning he's crouching

with one leg out in front of him and his hands in the air like he's sliding into home plate and winning the World Series of Disco.

"What the fuck?!? Hey, look out!" scream the riders as they break formation and scatter. Meanwhile, the roller skater is similarly annoyed, looking as though he'd traveled three hours to some roller rink only to find that it's closed for a floor rebuffing. Fortunately, nobody actually hit anybody else, but while a collision had been averted, it was only by the grace of the disco gods. Had one of the cyclists braked a nanosecond later, or had Rollerguy extended that *Saturday Night Fever* index finger just a few inches farther, then it doubtless would have taken the Jaws of Life to separate the twisted mass of carbon, roller skates, and white man Afro.

In this situation, the force that was at work is called "Social Onanism." Basically, onanism means "masturbation," so social onanism refers to any situation in which a person or a single group is engaged in a completely self-serving activity that inconveniences others. Here are a few common examples of social onanism:

- Cycling at high speed through a crowded park in the middle of the day;
- Engaging in wild roller-discoing in a crowded park in the middle of the day;
- Getting way too into the music on your headphones on the subway and singing or rapping out loud (doubly onanistic if the lyrics are obscene);
- Erratic or reckless cycling, driving, or even walking (yes, I've seen people engaged in "fancy walking");

- Talking on your cell phone really loudly because you secretly enjoy letting strangers know about your important job, lavish purchases, and high-powered lifestyle.

Isolated instances of social onanism are annoying, but when two or more socially onanistic people or groups encounter each other, the effect multiplies exponentially—this is the Social Onanism Synergistic Effect. The group of speeding Freds is one thing, but when you throw Rollerguy into the mix, the situation becomes far more dangerous, and had the weird guy with the rubber ball suddenly appeared on the scene, there would almost certainly have been utter carnage. Furthermore, social onanism doesn't just apply to recreational setting such as parks. It also extends to the commute, an arena defined by its onanism.

We will never eliminate social onanism from our society—nor would we want to. As irritating as it is, social onanism can sometimes be extremely entertaining, and I wouldn't want to live in a world without people like Rollerguy. Just as there's good cholesterol and bad cholesterol, there's also good social onanism and bad social onanism. To some extent, what constitutes good and bad social onanism is in the eye of the beholder, but generally speaking the more "flambullient" it is, the better it is, since its goodness is defined by its entertainment value. (An objective bystander would probably be far more entertained by Rollerguy than by the speeding Freds.)

On the high seas, there are strict rules that govern which boat shall have the right-of-way, and obviously similar rules also govern our streets. However, there are no rules that tell us how to behave when we encounter social onanism, which is, by its nature, totally unpredictable.

In short, which freak has the right of way?

I maintain that the safest course of action, regardless of speed or vehicle, is to always defer to the more flambullient party. Even though the speeding Freds are going faster and there are more of them, Rollerguy can't reasonably be expected to incorporate evasive action into his syncopated disco moves.

Likewise, unless you're genuinely and irresistibly flambullient, you should probably avoid social onanism. If you're unsure as to whether you qualify, here's a good test: While you were being socially onanistic, has anyone ever tried to give you money? If so, then you're up there with the street performers, so by all means continue. If not, you may want to give it up and keep to singing in the shower like the rest of us.

CONFESS!!!

It can be painful yet relieving to get something off your chest. No, I'm not talking about waxing that Alec Baldwin throw rug or tweezing unsightly nipple hair. I'm talking about the cathartic and spiritually edifying act of confession.

In the best possible world, commuting would be like good sex: an essential part of life we nonetheless engage in with pleasure. Unfortunately, in the real world, commuting is like *bad* sex: a drudgery we engage in out of a sense of duty or else a series of misguided impulses that leaves us feeling tremendously guilty afterward.

It has been said that guilt is a useless emotion. This is completely untrue. Guilt is an extremely important emotion because:

1. It can be used as a powerful weapon. (Making friends, family members, and loved ones feel guilty can lead them to furnish you with goods and services at no financial cost to you.)

2. It can let you know when you're behaving poorly, or being what is technically referred to as an "asshole."

If you've ever felt guilty after commuting, this could be a sign that you're doing it wrong. Basically, there are two reasons people might experience guilt after commuting:

1. They feel bad about their choice of vehicle.
2. They realize, in retrospect, that they behaved like an asshole.

As far as feeling bad about vehicle choice, this is generally experienced by the sorts of smug people who feel that one kind vehicle is more righteous than another. Generally speaking, among the smug, vehicles can be broken down into two groups: Good and Evil. "Good" vehicles are many, and they include:

- Bicycles.
- Trains.
- Motor vehicles powered by alternative fuels such as electricity, vegetable oil, or the driver's own cloying sense of self-satisfaction.
- Canoes, kayaks, rowboats, sampans, sailboats, and other vessels powered by people or the wind.
- Organically fed horses.
- Anything inconvenient.

"Bad" vehicles, on the other hand, are simply any that satisfy the following criterion:

- Has an engine that burns gasoline. (The only known exception to this criterion is those boats environmentalists use to harass whalers and oil derricks.)

Even some "Good" vehicles are better than others. For example, while most bicycles are good, a creaky and misshapen bamboo bicycle you made yourself at some sort of local cooperative where they also teach classes like "urban beekeeping" trumps almost any bicycle in terms of sheer righteousness. However, the truth is that there are no such things as "Bad" vehicles—there are only bad vehicle operators. And by "Bad" I mean "stupid." A truck that burns gasoline is not a bad or stupid vehicle at all, but a person who uses that truck to travel like half a mile on smooth pavement without carrying anything is probably stupid, mostly because he or she is going to wind up sitting in traffic for no good reason and wasting a bunch of money and time in the process.

Conversely, sometimes you need a gasoline-burning truck—like when you do have to carry something over a long distance. All of us have used a truck in this way at one time or another, whether it's driving one or simply receiving a delivery from one. However, the sorts of people who believe in "Good" and "Bad" vehicles can't do this without giving a lengthy explanation of why they did it, and how they never ever do it except for this one time, and how they totally would have moved their living room set across town with their misshapen bamboo bicycle if only they weren't still sore from that whole swarm of bees mishap at the urban honey-making cooperative, and so forth.

They feel guilty, though like the masturbator there's no real reason for them to feel guilty, and really, the only offense they're committing is talking about what they should be keeping (not bee-keeping) to themselves.

However, the other form of guilt, where you realize you were being an asshole, is the more significant one. This occurs when, instead of thinking one vehicle is superior to another, you take it a step further and believe that *you* are superior to another person—which reduces you to nothing more than a crotch irritant, regardless of the other person's perceived or actual infraction.

I know I said that cyclists are the Chosen Commuters, but that's not because we're better. Really, it's mostly an accident, like getting called for jury duty. Actually, we're all more or less equally stupid—it's just that some of us don't *realize* we're being stupid, which is the worst form of stupidity. This unwitting stupidity might be cutting someone off because you were texting while driving or it might be kicking someone's car because they cut you off because they were texting while driving. The most insidious thing about being stupid is that stupidity begets stupidity, and it can be very easy to fall into a sort of "Feedback Loop of Idiocy." At best, two people embarrass themselves, and at worst, someone gets hurt in a fight over a situation in which nobody got hurt. Alas, when we are wronged it is all too easy to get carried away in the heat of the moment, or *in flagrante indignito*, or whatever you want to call it. This is probably the hardest part of being a cyclist—our patience and composure must be equal to our vulnerability and the amount of indignity to which we are subjected.

The worst part, after the argument is over, is that the righteousness that boiled over into anger eventually simmers down, and by the time you get to your destination, it's congealed into that gooey, vaguely nauseating pot of goop known as "guilt."

We've all heard Jesus's famous admonition: "Let he who is without sin cast the first stone." It's good advice, but it's also been around for like two thousand years and it's still not helping, since most of us go around hurling figurative stones at each other like politicians throwing out the first pitch at a baseball game. Also, this bit of advice has a lot of gravity when you're talking about chucking rocks at the Son of God, but when your target is just some porcine schmuck in a Buick and your rock is a nice hefty insult like "Cocksucker!" or "Watch where you're going, motherfucker!" it's a lot harder to exercise restraint.

We can, however, embrace those embarrassing moments—those guilt-inducing losses of self-control—by confessing them, and each one of us has just such a moment. One that haunts me is the time I was riding along the bike lane of a busy street in Brooklyn, and just ahead of me was a Toyota Prius.

In the "Good" and "Bad" vehicle smugness spectrum, the Prius inhabits sort of a gray area. It's "Good" because it's partially electric, which allows people to congratulate themselves for driving it, but it's "Bad" because it still burns gasoline. In this sense it's like the guy who works on Wall Street but thinks the tribal ankle band he hides under his dress sock makes him "alternative." In the Gnostic view, it's the "Psychic" of vehicles.

In any case, like many people I already carry a lot of emotional baggage where the Prius is concerned, but on top of this the driver of this particular Prius was engaged in an intense texting session on his BlackBerry or similar handheld smart-phone device, which he operated with both hands while steering with his knees. Consequently, every few feet, he'd veer into the bike lane like it was a stream and he was a smug, hybrid-powered wildebeest occasionally sipping from it.

This was quite assuredly upper echelon moron behavior. At the same time, I was in no immediate danger since traffic was moving quite slowly and I could easily anticipate and avoid his idiotic weavings. Still, every time he swerved, my smoldering anger grew hotter, and as I watched him typing away with his thumbs (opposable, amazingly—I would not have thought him so highly evolved) with a total lack of consideration in his dainty little smugmobile I finally lost it, stuck my head in his open passenger side window, and yelled, "Boo!"

Roughly four blocks later this had escalated into a sad shouting match in which some bonehead in a Prius and a self-righteous bike dork both dared each other to leave their respective vehicles and fight, even though each of us clearly didn't want to, though we couldn't admit we didn't want to for fear of forfeiting—thus ensuring that the Feedback Loop of Idiocy would continue unbroken, until one of us finally felt as though he had hurled the insult that would qualify as the "last word."

By the time I got home, I was thoroughly and profoundly humiliated by my behavior.

I confess this to you now in the hope that you too will confess your commuting sins—and I know you have them. I also know that cyclists can be as bad as anybody.

I have watched the timid Nü-Fred strike with soft, moisturized fist the taxi that didn't really get particularly close to him.

I have watched the smug self-appointed transit advocate berate a police officer for not standing at the foot of the Manhattan Bridge bike lane and warning approaching cyclists of a small patch of ice.

I have watched the commuter run a red light and then curse out the driver who almost hit him.

And all too often I've been these people, or at least shades of these people, and the memories of these instances and the resulting guilt has kept me lying awake at night for as long as two minutes before I cast it aside, muttered, "Eh, whatever," and drifted into a contented slumber.

So confess! Let us unburden ourselves of our commuting sins like a member of the local food co-op emptying his panniers of locally grown, organic produce. Let us admit that as cyclists we can be, and often are, annoying. Let us set off on every commute resolved not to have a hissy fit, for if we cannot succeed in this regard, then verily we are no better than the person who cannot get through a date without surreptitiously placing his companion's hand in his crotch. Let us usher in a glorious new age of silent and graceful nobility.

"Tend to your garden," went the central message of Voltaire's *Candide*, and even though I got like an 82 on that test, I always took this little bit of advice to heart. Most of us tend to our jobs and our families and our homes and our social lives with love and dedication, but it's too easy to neglect the footpaths between these gardens and let them get overgrown. We need to tend to these gardens too, though not by hacking away at the foliage with a machete or a U-lock, but with care and patience. We need to learn to enjoy our journey along these shared paths as much as we enjoy the time spent in our various flower beds and greenhouses once we get there, and to make the best of our interactions with the people we pass along the way:

"PASSING Stranger!" wrote Walt Whitman,

"You do not know how longingly I look upon you,

You must be he I was seeking, or she I was seeking, (it comes to me, as of a dream)

I have somewhere surely lived a life of joy with you..."

That seems as good a way to treat a stranger as any, as we all make our way along the Dachshund of Time.

Anyway, it sure beats calling him a cocksucker.

ACKNOWLEDGEMENTS

I'm extremely fortunate to have a great agent in Danielle Svetcov at the Levine Greenberg Literary Agency and a great editor in Emily Haynes at Chronicle Books. Thanks to them my "job" is easy. Deepest thanks also to Emilie Sandoz, April Whitney, and everybody at Chronicle for their expertise and hard work. Most of all, thanks to my readers for continuing to humor me, and for affording me the incredible privilege of being a writer. I feel lucky every day.

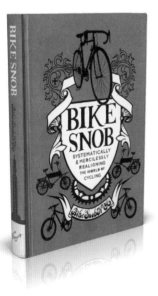